101 Stovetop SUPPERS

Barbecue Chicken Kabobs, page 7   *Maryland Crab Cakes, page 87*   *Too-Much-Zucchini Stovetop Dinner, page 26*

Gooseberry Patch
2500 Farmers Dr., #110
Columbus, OH 43235

www.gooseberrypatch.com
1·800·854·6673

Copyright 2013, Gooseberry Patch 978-1-62093-029-8
First Printing, June, 2013

All rights reserved. No part of this book may be reproduced or utilized in any form or by any means, electronic or mechanical, including photocopying and recording, or by any information storage and retrieval system, without permission in writing from the publisher. Printed in India.

Check out our cooking videos on YouTube!

Scan this code with your smartphone or tablet...it takes you right to our YouTube playlist of cooking videos for **101 Stovetop Suppers**. While there, you can also view our entire collection of **Gooseberry Patch** cooking videos!

If you spot this icon next to a recipe name, it means we created a video for it. You'll find it at **www.youtube.com/gooseberrypatchcom**

Gooseberry Patch *cookbooks*

Farmhouse Pork & Cabbage Sauté, page 48

Chicken & Snow Pea Stir-Fry, page 21

Since 1992, we've been publishing our own country cookbooks for every kitchen and for every meal of the day! Each title has hundreds of budget-friendly recipes, using ingredients you already have on hand in your pantry.

In addition, you'll find helpful tips and ideas on every page, along with our hand-drawn artwork and plenty of personality. Their lay-flat binding makes them so easy to use...they're sure to become a fast favorite in your kitchen.

Call us toll-free at
1•800•854•6673
and we'd be delighted to tell you all about our newest titles!

Shop with us online anytime at
www.gooseberrypatch.com

Send us your favorite recipe!

and the memory that makes it special for you! If we select your recipe for a brand-new **Gooseberry Patch** cookbook, your name will appear right along with it...and you'll receive a FREE copy of the book!

Submit your recipe on our website at
www.gooseberrypatch.com

Or mail to:
Gooseberry Patch • Attn: Cookbook Dept.
2500 Farmers Dr., #110 • Columbus, OH 43235

Please include the number of servings and all other necessary information!

Have a taste for more?

Visit **www.gooseberrypatch.com** to join our **Circle of Friends**!

- Free recipes, tips and ideas plus a complete cookbook index
- Get special email offers and our monthly eLetter delivered to your inbox
- Find local stores with **Gooseberry Patch** cookbooks, calendars and organizers

Chicken Romano, page 9

Chocolate Oatmeal Cookies, page 46

Speedy Chicken Gumbo, page 84

Taco in a Pan, page 85

Creole Pork Chops & Rice, page 40

Simple Skillet Peaches, page 106

Fajitas with Grilled Vegetables, page 63

CONTENTS

Quick & Easy 7

Slowly Simmered 48

Serves a Crowd..................... 84

Spicy Sausage & Rice, page 15

Dedication

For everyone who loves to serve a homemade dinner around the table, but doesn't have all day to spend in the kitchen!

Appreciation

To all those busy cooks who sent us your best one-dish stovetop recipes...we can't thank you enough!

Dijon Beef Stew, page 57

Barbecue Chicken Kabobs

4 boneless, skinless chicken
   breasts, cubed
1 green pepper, cut into 2-inch
   squares
1 sweet onion, cut into wedges
1 red pepper, cut into 2-inch
   squares
1 c. favorite barbecue sauce
4 to 6 skewers

Thread chicken, green pepper, onion
and red pepper pieces alternately
onto skewers. Place kabobs on a
lightly oiled grill pan over medium
heat. Cook for 12 to 15 minutes,
turning and brushing frequently with
barbecue sauce, until chicken juices
run clear and vegetables are tender.
Serves 4 to 6.

Robin Hill
Rochester, NY

As soon as our local farmers'
market opens, I look for my
"chicken lady." She brings
the freshest, most flavorful
chicken for these kabobs.

One-Dish Speedy Couscous

12-oz. pkg. couscous, uncooked
2 c. cooked chicken, diced
1 zucchini, chopped
1 stalk celery, thinly sliced
1 carrot, peeled and grated
2 c. orange juice
1/4 c. fresh basil, chopped
2 green onions, finely chopped
1/2 t. salt
1/2 t. pepper

Combine couscous, chicken and vegetables in a large serving bowl; set aside. Bring orange juice to a boil in a saucepan over medium heat; stir into couscous mixture. Cover tightly with plastic wrap; let stand for 5 minutes. Sprinkle with remaining ingredients. Stir gently until evenly mixed. Serves 4.

Laurel Perry
Loganville, GA

This hearty and flavorful meal is ready in a flash! The orange juice adds a nice zing...plus it's a great way to use up leftover chicken.

Chicken Romano

**Krysta Bickley
Alliance, OH**

These juicy, breaded chicken cutlets are perfect served over cooked pasta, topped with some sauce, shredded mozzarella and a sprinkle of Parmesan cheese.

3 T. Italian-flavored dry bread crumbs
3 T. grated Pecorino-Romano cheese
1 lb. chicken cutlets
1 T. olive oil, divided
14-1/2 oz. can diced tomatoes, drained and 1/3 c. juice reserved
3 cloves garlic, pressed
2 T. Kalamata olives
1 t. balsamic vinegar
1/8 t. red pepper flakes
3 T. fresh basil, chopped

9

Combine bread crumbs and cheese in a shallow dish. Dredge chicken pieces in bread crumb mixture until coated on both sides. Heat oil in a large skillet over medium heat. Working in batches, add 2 chicken cutlets. Cook, turning once, for about 10 minutes, until golden on both sides and no longer pink in the center. Remove from skillet and keep warm. Add tomatoes, garlic, olives, vinegar, red pepper flakes and reserved tomato juice to skillet. Cook for 2 minutes, stirring occasionally, or until slightly thickened. Remove from heat and discard garlic. Stir in basil. To serve, spoon sauce over chicken. Serves 4.

Basil & Tomato Soup ▶

2 T. oil
1 onion, chopped
2 to 3 tomatoes, chopped
1-1/2 lbs. yellow squash, chopped
3 c. chicken broth
1 c. buttermilk
1/4 c. fresh basil, minced
Garnish: fresh basil sprigs

Heat oil in a skillet over medium heat. Sauté onion until tender, about 5 minutes. Add tomatoes and continue to cook for 5 minutes, or until tomatoes are soft. Stir in squash and chicken broth; bring to a boil. Reduce heat and simmer 15 minutes, or until squash is fork-tender. Working in batches, spoon mixture into a blender or food processor; purée with buttermilk until mixture is smooth. Sprinkle in basil; stir. Garnish servings with more fresh basil. Serves 6 to 8.

Vickie

Fresh basil is unsurpassed in summer dishes...it adds a spicy, flavorful goodness that can't be beat. Try it in this garden-fresh soup.

So-Easy Pork Fritters

1 lb. pork tenderloin, sliced
 1/2-inch thick
1 egg, beaten
3 T. milk
1 sleeve saltine crackers, finely
 crushed
3/4 c. all-purpose flour
1 t. salt
1/2 t. pepper
oil for frying

Flatten pork with a meat mallet;
set aside. Place egg and milk in a
small bowl and blend well. Combine
cracker crumbs, flour and seasonings
in a separate bowl. Dip pork slices
into egg mixture, then press in
crumb mixture until well coated.
Heat 1/2 inch of oil in a skillet over
medium-high heat. Add pork slices;
fry until deep golden on both sides
and no longer pink in the middle,
turning as needed. Serves 4.

Elena Nelson
Concordia, MO
This is my husband's favorite
meal. I created this recipe
to mimic a menu item at our
favorite restaurant. These
fritters are excellent
in a sandwich too.

Easy One-Pot Chicken & Rice

1 T. butter
2 10-oz. cans chicken, drained
1/2 c. chicken broth
15-oz. can mixed vegetables,
    partially drained
salt and pepper to taste
2 t. garlic salt
2 c. instant rice, uncooked
1/2 to 3/4 c. boiling water,
    divided
1/4 to 1/3 c. honey mustard

Melt butter in a skillet over medium-high heat. Add chicken and cook until heated through. Stir in broth and vegetables with remaining juice. Heat until boiling; add seasonings. Stir in rice and 1/2 cup water. Cover and remove from heat; let stand for about 5 minutes, until almost all the liquid has been absorbed. If rice is not tender, stir in another 1/4 cup water, cover and cook on medium heat until remaining liquid is absorbed. Stir in mustard. Serves 4.

Samantha Mireles
San Antonio, TX

This dish is so easy to toss together...and it tastes great too. The honey mustard adds a wonderful sweet & savory touch.

Family-Favorite Pork Tacos

2 t. oil
1-lb. pork tenderloin, cubed
1 t. ground cumin
2 cloves garlic, minced
1 c. green or red salsa
Optional: 1/2 c. fresh cilantro,
    chopped
8 10-inch corn tortillas, warmed
Garnish: shredded lettuce, diced
    tomatoes, sliced avocado,
    sliced black olives, sour cream,
    shredded Cheddar cheese

Heat oil in a skillet over medium-
high heat. Add pork and cumin;
cook until golden on all sides and
pork is no longer pink in the center,
about 8 to 10 minutes. Add garlic
and cook for one minute; drain.
Stir in salsa and heat through; stir
in cilantro, if using. Using 2 forks,
shred pork. Fill warmed tortillas with
pork mixture; garnish as desired.
Serves 4.

13

Carol Lytle
Columbus, OH

My kids liked to order
tacos just like these at
our neighborhood Mexican
restaurant, so I recreated
the recipe to make at home.

Skillet Chicken-Fried Rice

1 T. oil
2 eggs, beaten
1/2 c. frozen peas
1/2 c. carrot, peeled and sliced
1/4 c. onion, diced
2 c. cooked rice
1 c. cooked chicken, cubed
2 T. soy sauce
1 T. stir-fry sauce
1/4 t. garlic, minced

Heat oil in a large skillet over medium heat. Scramble eggs in oil. When eggs are set, remove from pan and chop. Lightly spray the same skillet with non-stick cooking spray and place over medium heat. Add peas, carrot and onion to skillet. Cook for 2 to 3 minutes, until vegetables are crisp-tender. Add chopped scrambled eggs and remaining ingredients to vegetable mixture. Cook, stirring occasionally, until mixture is heated through. Makes 4 servings.

Nicole Sampson
Tiskilwa, IL

This is a very easy one-skillet supper and it's oh-so delicious. Why order takeout when you can whip this up in no time flat?

Spicy Sausage & Rice

3-1/2 c. cooked rice
16-oz. pkg. smoked sausage links,
    sliced into bite-size pieces
8-oz. jar salsa
Garnish: diced green pepper,
    diced tomato, sliced japaleños

In a large skillet over medium heat, combine all ingredients except garnish. Cook, stirring occasionally, until sausage is heated through and most of the liquid is absorbed. Top servings with diced pepper, diced tomato and jalapeño slices. Makes 6 to 8 servings.

15

Brian Johnson
Columbus, OH

This spicy sausage dish is quick to make on busy evenings after a long day. It's so simple...just combine everything in one skillet and you're ready to eat!

Quick & Easy
Sloppy Cowboys

2 lbs. lean ground beef
1/2 t. dried oregano
1/2 t. dried basil
1/2 t. onion powder
1/3 t. garlic powder
0.7-oz. pkg. Italian salad
    dressing mix
1 T. red wine vinegar
1 t. Worcestershire sauce
1/3 c. catsup
sandwich buns
1/2 lb. provolone cheese, sliced

Brown beef in a large skillet over medium heat; drain. Add remaining ingredients except buns and cheese and mix well. Reduce heat to low; simmer until heated through and slightly thickened. Serve on buns, topped with a slice of provolone cheese. Serves 6 to 8.

Rachel Kowasic
Connellsville, PA
I found a recipe for Sloppy Joes, but they weren't quite what I wanted, so I turned them into my own special type of Sloppy Joe... Sloppy Cowboys!

Meatball Soup

14-1/2 oz. can petite diced
  tomatoes
6-oz. can tomato paste
1 to 1-1/2 c. onion, chopped
4 14-1/2 oz. cans beef broth
2 c. water
32-oz. pkg. frozen meatballs
1-1/2 c. orzo, ditalini or other
  small pasta, uncooked
salt and pepper to taste
Garnish: grated Parmesan cheese

Mix together all ingredients except garnish in a large stockpot over medium heat. Bring to a boil; reduce heat to medium-low. Cook, stirring occasionally, for 20 minutes, or until pasta is tender and meatballs are warmed through. Garnish servings with Parmesan cheese. Makes 6 to 8 servings.

Amber Belt
Lafayette, IN

We tried this recipe while camping because it was easy to toss together... we quickly learned that it was so good we'd be eating it a lot more often!

Garden Skillet Dinner with Chicken

1 lb. boneless skinless chicken
  breast, diced
1/4 c. all-purpose flour
1/3 c. olive oil
2 T. garlic, minced
1/2 c. red pepper, sliced
1/2 c. carrot, peeled and sliced
1/2 c. celery, sliced
1/2 c. broccoli flowerets
1 T. dried basil
3/4 c. chicken broth
3/4 c. whipping cream
12-oz. pkg. egg noodles, cooked
salt and pepper to taste

Combine chicken and flour in a
large plastic zipping bag. Shake until
chicken is evenly coated; discard
remaining flour. Heat oil in a large
skillet over medium heat. Sauté
chicken in oil until golden and no
longer pink in the center. Add
garlic, vegetables and basil; cook for
2 minutes. Reduce heat to low; stir in
broth and cream. When mixture has
thickened slightly, stir in noodles.
Heat through; season with salt and
pepper. Serves 4 to 6.

Jennie Gist
Gooseberry Patch

This is one-pot comfort
food at its finest...warm
chicken and vegetables over
noodles. Plus, clean-up is
quick as a wink!

Kickin' Cajun Tilapia

3 T. paprika
1 T. onion powder
1 t. cayenne pepper
1 t. dried thyme
1 t. dried oregano
1/2 t. celery salt
1/8 t. garlic powder
2 t. salt
2 t. pepper
4 tilapia fillets
2 T. oil
Garnish: lemon wedges

Mix seasonings in a shallow bowl or on a plate. Press both sides of tilapia fillets into seasoning mixture; let stand for 10 minutes. Heat oil in a skillet over medium heat. Cook fillets for 4 to 6 minutes, turning once, until fish flakes easily with a fork. Remove fish to a serving plate and garnish with lemon wedges. Serves 4.

19

Amanda Johnson
Marysville, OH
My husband loves this delicious fish dish! Tilapia is a mild, tasty fish, and this recipe really has a flavorful zip.

Shrimp & Orzo Salad

1-1/2 c. orzo pasta, uncooked
1 c. asparagus, trimmed and
   cut into bite-size pieces
1 c. cooked medium shrimp
3 green onions, thinly sliced
1/2 c. fresh parsley, chopped
Italian salad dressing to taste

Cook orzo according to package directions; drain and rinse with cold water. Place asparagus in a large saucepan of simmering water for 3 to 4 minutes. Drain and rinse with cold water. In a serving bowl, mix together orzo, asparagus, shrimp, onions and parsley. Drizzle with salad dressing; toss to mix. Serves 6.

Rosemary Lightbown
Wakefield, RI

Everyone loves this yummy salad. It's perfect for hot summer days when you don't want to heat up your kitchen too much.

Chicken & Snow Pea Stir-Fry

1 T. reduced-sodium soy sauce
1 t. chile-garlic or curry sauce
1 T. rice vinegar
2 t. toasted sesame oil
1/2 lb. boneless, skinless chicken
    breast, cubed
1 T. fresh ginger, peeled and
    minced
3 c. snow peas, trimmed
3 green onions, chopped
3 T. unsalted cashews, broken
cooked rice
Optional: additional chile-garlic
    sauce

Combine sauces and vinegar in a small bowl; set aside. Heat oil in a skillet over medium-high heat. Add chicken; cook and stir until no longer pink in the center. Add ginger; cook and stir for about 30 seconds. Add snow peas and onions; cook until snow peas are just tender, about 2 to 4 minutes. Add soy sauce mixture; stir to coat well. Stir in cashews just before serving. Serve over cooked rice; top with more chile-garlic sauce, if desired. Makes 3 to 4 servings.

Liz Plotnick-Snay
Gooseberry Patch

My husband and I are always looking for new chicken dishes. This recipe turned out delicious, especially with our own additions to it.

BBQ Shrimp & Pineapple Kabobs

8 uncooked large shrimp, peeled
   and cleaned
1 c. pineapple, cubed
1 green pepper, cut into 2-inch
   squares
1 sweet onion, cut into wedges
1/4 c. teriyaki barbecue sauce
4 skewers
cooked rice

Thread shrimp, pineapple, green
pepper and onion pieces alternately
onto skewers. Place kabobs on a
lightly oiled grill pan over medium
heat. Cook for 8 to 10 minutes,
turning and brushing frequently with
barbecue sauce, until shrimp are pink
and cooked through. Serve kabobs
over rice. Makes 4 servings.

Jen Stout
Blandon, PA

These are delightfully
different than the usual
steak or chicken kabobs. They
have a tropical taste that's
sure to make you feel like
you're soaking in the sun.

Rosemary Peppers & Fusilli

2 to 4 T. olive oil
2 red onions, thinly sliced and
　separated into rings
3 red, orange and/or yellow
　peppers, very thinly sliced
5 to 6 cloves garlic, very thinly
　sliced
3 T. dried rosemary
salt and pepper to taste
12-oz. pkg. fusilli pasta, cooked
Garnish: shredded mozzarella
　cheese

Add oil to a large skillet over
medium heat. Add onions to skillet;
cover and cook over medium heat
for 10 minutes. Stir in remaining
ingredients except pasta and cheese;
reduce heat. Cook, covered, stirring
occasionally, for an additional
20 minutes. Serve vegetable mixture
over pasta, topped with cheese.
Makes 4 servings.

23

Jennifer Niemi
Nova Scotia, Canada
This colorful, flavorful
meatless meal is ready to
serve in a jiffy. If you
can't find fusilli pasta,
try sea shells, rotini or
even wagon wheels.

Inside-Out Stuffed Pepper

1 green pepper, top removed
1 lb. ground beef
1 onion, chopped
1-1/2 c. cooked rice
8-oz. can tomato sauce
salt and pepper to taste

Bring a saucepan of salted water to a boil. Add green pepper and cook for 8 to 10 minutes, until tender. Drain; cool slightly and chop pepper. Meanwhile, cook beef and onion in a skillet over medium heat, stirring often, until beef is browned and onion is translucent. Drain; add green pepper and cooked rice to skillet. Pour tomato sauce over beef mixture; stir and heat through. Season with salt and pepper to taste. Serves 4.

Charlene McCain
Bakersfield, CA

A quick and tasty dish for those nights when you get home late and everybody's hungry...super-simple to toss together and satisfies even the biggest of hungers!

Quick & Easy
Saucy Beef Skillet

3 T. oyster sauce or soy sauce
1-1/2 T. dry sherry or orange
    juice
2 t. cornstarch
1/2 t. sugar
2 T. peanut oil
2 lbs. beef round steak, thinly
    sliced
6 green onions, sliced 1/2-inch
    long

In a bowl, mix together sauce, sherry or orange juice, cornstarch and sugar; set aside. Heat oil in a large skillet over medium heat; add steak and cook for about 3 minutes. Stir in sauce mixture. Add green onions and cook for an additional 10 minutes, or until steak is cooked through and onions are tender. Serves 4.

Dottie Liwai
Durant, OK

This beef comes out so tender...it's absolutely wonderful. Serve over some cooked rice or egg noodles and you've got yourself one tasty meal!

25

Too-Much-Zucchini Stovetop Dinner

2 T. olive oil
2 cloves garlic, minced
1 onion, chopped
1 lb. ground beef
1/2 lb. ground Italian pork
    sausage
3 to 4 zucchini, quartered and
    sliced 1/2-inch thick
26-oz. jar spaghetti sauce
14-1/2 oz. can crushed tomatoes
6-oz. can tomato paste
1/2 c. water
1/2 t. dried basil
1/2 t. dried oregano
1/2 t. garlic powder
salt and pepper to taste
8-oz. pkg. shredded mozarella
    cheese
3 c. elbow macaroni, cooked

Add oil to a skillet over medium heat. Sauté garlic and onion until tender, about 5 minutes. Add beef and sausage; cook until browned. Drain; add zucchini, sauce, tomatoes, tomato paste and water. Cover and simmer for 10 to 15 minutes, until zucchini is tender. Add seasonings; top with cheese. Serve over macaroni. Serves 6 to 8.

Maria Kuhns
Crofton, MD

This is a recipe my mom created when she had an overabundance of zucchini in her garden. I've been eating this since I was a little girl.

Vegetable Quesadillas

8-oz. pkg. reduced-fat shredded
  Cheddar or Monterey Jack
  cheese
1/4 c. onion, grated
15-oz. can corn, drained
15-oz. can black beans, drained
  and rinsed
8-oz. jar salsa
6 10-inch flour tortillas

In a bowl, combine all ingredients
except tortillas; mix well. Evenly
spoon mixture onto one half of
each tortilla; fold over and gently
press together. Working in batches,
place tortillas in a lightly greased
skillet over medium heat. Cook until
golden; flip and cook until other side
is golden. Slice into wedges to serve.
Serves 4 to 6.

27

Linda Neff
West Jefferson, OH
These quesadillas were a hit
at a "Family Cooks" night
at a local elementary school
recently. Serve with some
fresh salsa for dipping.

Hearty Red Beans & Rice

1 green pepper, chopped
1 onion, chopped
1/2 c. green onion, chopped
1/2 c. celery, chopped
2 T. fresh parsley, chopped
3 slices bacon, crisply cooked,
  crumbled and drippings
  reserved
1/2 lb. Polish or Kielbasa
  sausage, sliced
2 15-oz. cans kidney beans,
  drained and rinsed
6-oz. can tomato paste
2-oz. jar chopped pimentos,
  drained
2 T. catsup
1-1/2 t. Worcestershire sauce
1 t. chili powder
cooked rice

In a skillet over medium heat, sauté green pepper, onions, celery and parsley in reserved drippings until tender. Stir in bacon and remaining ingredients except rice. Reduce heat; cover and simmer until thickened, about 25 to 30 minutes. Serve over cooked rice. Serves 4.

Kerry Mayer
Dunham Springs, LA
A big bowl of this down-home favorite really hits the spot.

Sweet Skillet Ham Steaks & Apples

1/4 c. butter
1/3 c. brown sugar, packed
2-1/2 T. Dijon mustard
2 T. red onion, thinly sliced
2 Red Delicious apples, cored
   and sliced
1 lb. cooked ham steaks

Melt butter in a skillet over medium
heat; stir in brown sugar and
mustard. Add onion and apple to
skillet; stir to coat well. Add ham
steaks to skillet. Cover and cook for
10 to 15 minutes, until apples are
soft and ham is warmed through.
Serves 2.

Paige Miller
Mansfield, OH

This skillet supper is
delicious on a cool, crisp
fall night, especially when
served with a side of
crispy hashbrowns.

Basil-Broccoli Pasta

6 T. olive oil
2 T. butter
4 cloves garlic, sliced
1 bunch broccoli, sliced into
    flowerets
1 c. chicken broth
16-oz. pkg. rigatoni pasta,
    cooked
2 T. fresh basil, chopped
pepper to taste
Optional: grated Parmesan
    cheese

Heat oil and butter in a skillet or
large saucepan over medium heat.
Add garlic; cook until lightly golden.
Add broccoli; increase heat to
medium-high. Cook and stir gently
until broccoli is almost tender, about
3 to 4 minutes. Pour in broth;
reduce heat and simmer until
broccoli is tender. Stir cooked pasta
into skillet; mix thoroughly and heat
through. Transfer to a serving dish;
top with remaining ingredients.
Serves 4 to 6.

Denise Bliss
Milton, NY

This can either be a yummy
side or a meatless main.
Broccoli is our favorite
vegetable...feel free to
add any veggie you like.

Amanda's Chicken & Orzo

4 T. olive oil, divided
4 boneless, skinless chicken
   breasts
1 t. dried basil
salt and pepper to taste
2 zucchini, sliced
8-oz. pkg. orzo pasta, uncooked
1 T. butter, softened
2 T. red wine vinegar
Optional: 1 t. fresh dill, snipped
Garnish: lemon wedges

Heat 2 tablespoons oil in a skillet over medium heat. Sprinkle chicken with basil, salt and pepper. Add chicken to skillet and cook, turning once, for 12 minutes, or until juices run clear. Remove chicken to a plate and keep warm. Add zucchini to skillet and cook for 3 minutes, or until crisp-tender. Meanwhile, cook orzo according to package directions; drain and stir in butter. Whisk together remaining oil, vinegar and dill, if using; drizzle over orzo and toss to mix. Season with additional salt and pepper, if desired. Serve chicken and zucchini with orzo, garnished with lemon wedges. Serves 4.

31

Cathy Gearheart
Narrows, VA

A great meal in about 20 minutes. This was a staple when my daughter was involved in sports and needed a light, quick, nutritious meal before a game.

Quick & Easy
Zucchini & Seashells Soup

4 c. vegetable broth
2 carrots, peeled and chopped
1 onion, chopped
1 c. small shell pasta, uncooked
2 zucchini, grated
salt and pepper to taste

In a large saucepan, bring broth to a boil over medium heat. Add carrots and onion; simmer for 10 minutes. Add pasta and zucchini. Simmer for 8 to 10 minutes, until tender. Season with salt and pepper. Makes 4 to 6 servings.

Judy Parks
Georgetown, TX
With this delicious recipe, you'll always know what to do with those extra zucchini. This soup is amazing reheated...if you have any leftover, that is!

Southwest Smoked Sausage Skillet

2 t. oil
14-oz. pkg. smoked chicken
   sausage, sliced 1/2-inch thick
1 zucchini, sliced
2 c. frozen corn with diced
   peppers and onions, thawed
15-oz. can black beans, drained
   and rinsed
2 c. cooked rice
1/2 c. salsa
1 t. chili powder
Garnish: 1 c. shredded Mexican-
   blend cheese, chopped fresh
   cilantro

Heat oil in a skillet over medium
heat. Sauté sausage, zucchini and
corn in oil for about 8 minutes,
until vegetables are cooked and
heated through. Stir in remaining
ingredients except garnish. Cook,
stirring occasionally, for 5 minutes,
or until hot. Garnish with cheese and
cilantro just before serving. Serves 6.

Steve Payerle
Dublin, OH

My uncle, who was from
New Mexico, taught me how to
make this dish. He always
used to make this when we
went camping.

Quick & Easy
Sole in Dill Butter

1/4 c. butter, softened
1 t. dill weed
1/2 t. onion powder
1/2 t. garlic powder
Optional: 1/2 t. salt
1/4 t. white pepper
2 lbs. sole fillets
Garnish: additional dill weed,
  lemon wedges

Blend together butter and seasonings in a small bowl. Transfer to a cast-iron skillet; heat over medium heat until butter mixture is melted. Add fish fillets to skillet. Cook for 3 to 4 minutes on each side, until fish flakes easily with a fork. Serve with desired garnishes. Serves 6.

Evelyn Love
Standish, ME

Serve with steamed broccoli for a quick & easy light meal. Other whitefish like cod or tilapia taste great in this recipe too!

Ramen Skillet Supper

1 lb. ground beef
2-1/2 c. water
2 3-oz. pkgs. beef-flavor ramen
    noodles with seasoning packets
1/2 c. stir-fry sauce
3 c. frozen stir-fry vegetables

Brown beef in a large skillet over
medium heat; drain. Add water,
one soup seasoning packet, sauce
and vegetables; bring to a boil.
Reduce heat to medium-low; cover
and cook, stirring occasionally, for
5 minutes, or until vegetables are
crisp-tender. Break up noodles; add
to skillet. Cover and cook, stirring
occasionally, 5 to 8 minutes, until
sauce is thickened and noodles are
tender. Serves 4.

Wendy Jacobs
Idaho Falls, ID

This is one of my go-to meals
for dinners after hectic days
of work and school. My
daughter Emma loves this
dish, and I love making it
because it's so simple.

Beef & Bean Tostadas

1 lb. ground beef
1/2 c. onion, finely diced
1-1/4 oz. pkg. taco seasoning mix
1 c. water
15-oz. can nacho cheese sauce
15-oz. can refried beans
6 corn tostada shells
Garnish: pico de gallo or salsa

Brown beef and onion in a skillet over medium heat; drain. Add taco seasoning and water; cook, stirring occasionally, for 5 to 7 minutes, until thickened. Meanwhile, place cheese sauce and beans in separate microwave-safe bowls. Heat, stirring occasionally, until warmed through. Spread tostada shells evenly with beans; top each with about 1/4 cup beef mixture. Drizzle with cheese sauce; garnish with pico de gallo or salsa. Serves 6.

Krista Marshall
Fort Wayne, IN
Kids will love this crunchy eat-with-your-hands supper. Tostadas are like an open-faced taco...great for Mexican-themed parties!

Stovetop Beef & Shells

1 lb. ground beef
1 onion, chopped
1 clove garlic, minced
15-oz. can crushed tomatoes
8-oz. can tomato sauce
1 t. sugar
1/2 t. salt
1/2 t. pepper
1/2 c. medium shell pasta,
   cooked

In a large saucepan over medium heat, brown beef, onion and garlic; drain. Stir in tomatoes with juice, tomato sauce, sugar, salt and pepper. Bring to a boil; reduce heat and simmer, uncovered, for 10 to 15 minutes. Add pasta to beef mixture; stir to mix. Serves 4.

**Mary Patenaude
Griswold, CT**
A heaping bowl of this savory pasta dish served with a thick slice of crusty Italian bread is a perfect dinner when you need something tasty and simple.

Pasta Puttanesca

3 to 6 cloves garlic, chopped
1/8 t. red pepper flakes
1/3 c. olive oil
2 15-oz. cans diced tomatoes,
    drained
1/8 t. dried oregano
1/4 c. dried parsley
3.8-oz. can chopped black olives,
    drained
8-oz. pkg. spaghetti, cooked
Garnish: grated Parmesan cheese

In a skillet over medium heat, sauté garlic and red pepper flakes in oil until golden. Add tomatoes and oregano. Reduce heat to low and simmer for 20 minutes, stirring occasionally. Stir in parsley and olives; cook for another 2 minutes. Add pasta to skillet; toss to mix and transfer to a large serving bowl. Sprinkle with cheese. Makes 4 servings.

**Christina Mattea
Oldsmar, FL**

This recipe was taught to me by my grandmother. It was always a dish she cooked in a pinch...it's quick, inexpensive and magnificent!

Stroganoff-Style Steak

1 lb. beef cube steak, quartered
salt and pepper to taste
1 T. oil
1.35-oz. pkg. onion soup mix
1 cube beef bouillon
1 c. boiling water
1/2 c. fat-free sour cream
Optional: 1/4 c. sliced
   mushrooms
cooked egg noodles or mashed
   potatoes

Season steak with salt and pepper.
Heat oil in a skillet over medium-
high heat. Add steak and brown on
both sides. In a bowl, combine
soup mix, bouillon cube and boiling
water; stir until bouillon is dissolved.
Pour over steak and reduce heat
to low. Cover and simmer for
15 minutes, or until steak is no
longer pink in the center. Add sour
cream and mushrooms, if using; cook
for 5 minutes, or until mushrooms
are tender. Serve over egg noodles
or mashed potatoes. Serves 4.

Marilyn Westendorf
Tampa, FL
Beef Stroganoff is one of my
husband's favorites, so I
came up with this recipe as
a fast alternative...great
for those evenings when
you don't have much time.

39

Creole Pork Chops & Rice

4 pork chops
1 T. oil
1 c. onion, diced
1 c. celery, diced
1 c. long-cooking rice, uncooked
29-oz. can tomato sauce
15-oz. can diced tomatoes
salt and pepper to taste

In a skillet over medium heat, cook pork chops in oil until golden but not cooked through. Add onion, celery and uncooked rice; stir in remaining ingredients. Reduce heat to low. Cover and simmer until rice is tender, about 15 to 20 minutes, adding water as needed to prevent drying out. Makes 4 servings.

Phyllis Covington
Guthrie, KY

This flavorful one-pot meal really smells amazing as it cooks...even the leftovers taste wonderful! It's yummy made with boneless, skinless chicken breasts too.

Ziti with Sausage & Zucchini

3/4 lb. ground Italian pork
   sausage
3 zucchini, thinly sliced
salt and pepper to taste
28-oz. can whole tomatoes
1/8 t. sugar
16-oz. pkg. ziti pasta, cooked
Garnish: grated Parmesan cheese

Brown sausage in a skillet over
medium heat; drain, reserving
one tablespoon drippings in skillet.
Add zucchini to skillet; season with
salt and pepper. Sauté until zucchini
is tender and golden, about
10 minutes. Stir in tomatoes with
juice and sugar; bring to a boil,
breaking up tomatoes with a spoon.
Return sausage to skillet and reduce
heat to low. Cover and cook until
heated through, about 5 to
6 minutes. Serve over pasta; sprinkle
with Parmesan cheese. Serves 6.

41

Sandra Sullivan
Aurora, CO

The whole family will
love this simple supper...
perfect with a slice of
crusty bread!

Hallie's Skillet Dried Beef & Corn

1 t. butter
2-1/2 oz. jar dried beef, chopped
2 T. onion, finely chopped
1 T. all-purpose flour
3/4 c. milk
15-oz. can creamed corn
2 T. green pepper, diced
3/4 c. shredded sharp Cheddar
   cheese
cornbread squares or toast slices

Melt butter in a skillet over medium heat. Sauté dried beef and onion in butter until beef begins to curl; stir in flour, mixing well. Add milk; cook and stir until thickened. Add corn and heat through. Stir in green pepper and cheese; cook over low heat until cheese melts. Spoon over cornbread or toast to serve. Serves 4.

Emily Johnson
Lyons, IN

My sister Hallie gave me this recipe years ago. She's no longer with us, but she looks over my shoulder each time I fix this scrumptious meal.

One-Pot Spicy Black Bean Chili

1 onion, chopped
2 t. garlic, minced
2 t. olive oil
3 15-oz. cans black beans,
    drained and rinsed
16-oz. pkg. frozen corn
10-oz. can tomatoes with chiles
1/2 c. water
1-1/2 t. taco seasoning mix
7-oz. can chipotle chiles in
    adobo sauce
1 T. rice vinegar
1/4 c. fresh cilantro, chopped
Garnish: sour cream, salsa,
    fresh cilantro sprigs

In a saucepan over medium heat,
sauté onion and garlic in oil for
5 to 7 minutes, until softened. Add
beans, corn, tomatoes, water and taco
seasoning. Bring to a boil; reduce
heat to low and simmer for about
15 minutes, stirring occasionally.
Combine chiles in sauce and vinegar
in a blender; process until puréed.
Stir chile mixture and cilantro into
chili; heat through. Garnish servings
as desired. Makes 4 servings.

43

Lisanne Miller
Canton, MS
Serve with crunchy tortilla
chips or a pan of warm
cornbread. If you like
a milder chili, just use
half of the chipotle
chile mixture.

Honey Chicken & Carrots

Coleen Lambert
Luxemburg, WI
This takes about 15 minutes to make and is so good. Whip up some instant rice for a side, and dinner is ready in the blink of an eye!

1 T. oil
4 boneless, skinless chicken
  breasts
1-1/2 c. carrots, peeled and sliced
2 T. honey
1 T. lemon juice
1/4 t. garlic salt
salt and pepper to taste
cooked rice

Heat oil in a skillet over medium heat. Add chicken; cook until golden on both sides and juices run clear, about 10 minutes. Remove chicken from skillet; keep warm. Add carrots to the same skillet; cook for 3 to 5 minutes, until tender. Stir in honey, lemon juice and garlic salt. Return chicken to skillet. Add salt and pepper to taste; heat through. To serve, spoon over cooked rice. Serves 4.

Pepperoni Tortellini

2 t. olive oil
1 onion, sliced
1 red pepper, thinly sliced
3 to 4 cloves garlic, chopped
5-oz. pkg. sliced pepperoni,
   cut into strips
1-1/2 t. dried basil
1-1/2 t. dried oregano
1 t. Italian seasoning
1 t. garlic powder
1/2 t. salt
1/4 t. pepper
8-oz. pkg. refrigerated 3-cheese
   tortellini pasta, cooked
Garnish: shaved Parmesan
   cheese, fresh basil

Heat oil in a skillet over medium heat. Sauté onion, red pepper and garlic until crisp-tender. Add remaining ingredients except pasta and garnish. Cook, stirring occasionally, for 5 minutes. Stir in pasta and cook until heated through. Garnish with Parmesan cheese and basil. Serves 4 to 6.

45

Eileen Boomgaarden
Waukesha, WI
I invented this recipe after I was newly married. It's fancy enough for adults, but fun and tasty enough for kids. Happy eating!

Chocolate Oatmeal Cookies

1/3 c. butter, melted
2 c. sugar
1/2 c. milk
1/3 c. baking cocoa
1 t. vanilla extract
1/2 c. creamy peanut butter
3 c. quick-cooking oats,
   uncooked

In a saucepan over medium heat, combine butter, sugar, milk and cocoa. Bring to a boil; cook for one minute. Remove from heat; stir in remaining ingredients. Mix well; drop by rounded teaspoonfuls onto wax paper. Let cookies cool completely. Makes about 2 dozen.

Lesleigh Robinson
Brownsville, TN

I've been making these since I was ten years old. They are the simplest cookies I've ever made...you don't even have to bake them!

Skillet Strawberry Jam

4 c. strawberries, hulled
   and crushed
1/2 c. sugar
1 T. lemon juice
Optional: 1/4 t. vanilla extract

Combine strawberries, sugar and
lemon juice in a skillet over medium-
high heat; mix well. Cook, stirring
often, until strawberries soften and
mixture thickens, about 10 minutes.
Remove from heat; stir in vanilla,
if using. Store in an airtight jar in
refrigerator for up to 3 weeks.
Makes about 1-1/2 cups.

47

Megan Brooks
Antioch, TN

This super-simple skillet
jam is delectable spread
on a freshly-baked homemade
biscuit or a toasty
English muffin.

Slowly Simmered
Farmhouse Pork & Cabbage Sauté

4 pork loin chops
1/4 t. salt, divided
1/8 t. pepper, divided
6 slices bacon, crisply cooked,
　crumbled and drippings
　reserved
1 t. olive oil
1 onion, thinly sliced
16-oz. pkg. shredded coleslaw mix
2 Golden Delicious apples, cored
　and sliced
3/4 lb. redskin potatoes, cubed
3/4 c. apple cider
1/4 t. dried thyme
1 T. cider vinegar

Season pork with salt and pepper; set aside. Heat reserved bacon drippings and oil in a Dutch oven over medium-high heat. Cook pork until golden on both sides, about 8 minutes. Remove pork and keep warm. Add onion to pan. Cover and cook over medium heat for 8 to 10 minutes, stirring occasionally, until golden. Gradually stir in coleslaw; cook until wilted, about 5 minutes. Add remaining ingredients except vinegar; bring to a boil. Reduce heat; cover and simmer for 15 minutes, until potatoes are tender. Stir in vinegar; return pork to pan and heat through. Sprinkle with reserved bacon. Makes 4 servings.

Jo Ann
I wanted to try something different from the usual cabbage rolls, so I whipped up this tasty recipe. What an amazing blend of flavors...it's now one of my family's favorites!

Pasta a la Drini

16-oz. pkg. Italian turkey sausage
   links
28-oz. can fire-roasted diced
   tomatoes
1/8 t. red pepper flakes
dried oregano and dried basil
   to taste
10-oz. pkg. frozen broccoli,
   cooked
16-oz. pkg. whole-wheat penne
   pasta, cooked

Place sausages on a grill pan over
medium heat. Cook until browned
and no longer pink in the center;
remove from pan and let cool. In a
large skillet over medium heat,
combine tomatoes with juice and
seasonings; bring to a simmer. Slice
sausages into bite-size pieces and
add to sauce. Add broccoli and pasta
to skillet. Return to a simmer and
cook for 3 to 5 minutes, until heated
through. Serves 4 to 6.

49

Catherine Alesandrini
French Village, MO
This is a great, healthy
one-pot meal that's on the
table in 30 minutes. It's
so versatile...add any
herbs or seasonings your
family likes.

Pulled Chicken & Slaw Sandwiches

1 c. favorite barbecue sauce
1 c. catsup
1/2 c. water
1 t. lemon juice
2/3 c. brown sugar, packed
1 deli roast chicken, boned and
   shredded
6 buns, split
Garnish: deli coleslaw

In a large saucepan, combine barbecue sauce, catsup, water, lemon juice and brown sugar. Stir well; add chicken. Cook over medium heat until mixture is heated through. Serve on buns; spoon slaw over chicken. Makes 6.

Barbara Cooper
Orion, IL

These sandwiches are super easy because you start with a roasted chicken from the deli. The creamy slaw adds a nice crunch...yum!

Slowly Simmered
Hearty Sausage Soup

1 T. olive oil
3 lbs. Kielbasa sausage, cut into
   bite-size pieces
3 onions, diced
3 cloves garlic, minced
3 16-oz. cans kidney beans,
   drained and rinsed
3 14-1/2 oz. cans diced
   tomatoes, drained
14-1/2 oz. can beef broth
1/2 c. long-cooking rice,
   uncooked
0.67-oz. pkg. fresh basil,
   chopped
1 t. Italian seasoning
1 t. dried oregano
1 t. dried parsley

Heat oil in a large stockpot over
medium heat. Add Kielbasa, onions
and garlic. Cook until golden; drain.
Add remaining ingredients; bring to
a boil over medium-high heat.
Reduce heat to low; simmer for
1-1/2 hours, stirring occasionally.
Makes 8 to 10 servings.

Wendy Dye
Monroe, NC
On cold nights, this soup is
a family favorite! Sometimes
we'll vary it by using part
Polish sausage or hot sausage
along with the Kielbasa.

Slowly Simmered
Skillet Goulash

2 lbs. ground beef
10-oz. can diced tomatoes with
   green chiles
6 baking potatoes, peeled
   and diced
15-oz. can tomato sauce
15-1/4 oz. can corn, drained
14-1/2 oz. can ranch-style beans
salt and pepper to taste

Brown beef in a Dutch oven over
medium heat; drain. Add tomatoes
with juice and remaining ingredients;
reduce heat. Cover and simmer until
potatoes are tender and mixture has
thickened, about 45 minutes. Makes
8 to 10 servings.

Kari Hodges
Jacksonville, TX

I like to serve up this
old-fashioned family favorite
with thick slices of freshly
baked sweet cornbread
topped with pats of butter.

One-Pot Beef Ravioli

1 lb. lean ground beef
1 t. oil
1 onion, diced
8-oz. pkg. sliced mushrooms
2 cloves garlic, minced
2 26-oz. jars tomato-basil
    pasta sauce
1 c. water
1 T. Italian seasoning
1/2 t. salt
1/4 t. pepper
20-oz. pkg. refrigerated 4-cheese
    ravioli
1 c. shredded mozzarella cheese

Brown beef in a Dutch oven over medium-high heat; drain and set beef aside in a bowl. Add oil to Dutch oven; sauté onion and mushrooms for 8 minutes, or until tender. Add garlic and cook for one minute. Stir in beef, pasta sauce, water and seasonings; bring to a boil. Add ravioli to sauce; reduce heat to medium-low. Cover and simmer, stirring occasionally, for 8 to 10 minutes, until pasta is cooked. Stir in cheese. Serves 4.

53

Sarah Jose
Shreveport, LA
This recipe is the perfect solution for a busy weeknight! I can have this on the table in less than 30 minutes, and there's only one pot to wash!

Slowly Simmered
Buttermilk Fried Chicken

2-1/2 lbs. chicken
1 c. buttermilk
1 c. all-purpose flour
1-1/2 t. salt
1/2 t. pepper
oil for frying

Combine chicken and buttermilk
in a large bowl. Cover and refrigerate
for one hour. Meanwhile, combine
flour, salt and pepper in a large
plastic zipping bag. Drain chicken,
discarding buttermilk. Working in
batches, add chicken to bag and toss
to coat. Shake off excess flour and
let chicken rest for 15 minutes. Heat
1/4 inch of oil in a large skillet over
medium heat. Fry chicken in oil until
golden on all sides. Reduce heat to
medium-low; cover and simmer,
turning occasionally, for 40 to
45 minutes, until juices run clear.
Uncover and cook 5 minutes longer.
Serves 4 to 6.

Cyndi Little
Whitsett, NC

My daddy made amazing fried
chicken, but he passed away
when I was 12. It's taken me
a long time to make chicken
that I feel is almost as
good as his.

Slowly Simmered
Low-Country Shrimp Boil

6 qts. water
3/4 c. seafood seasoning
2 lbs. new redskin potatoes
2 lbs. smoked pork sausage, cut
   into 1-inch pieces
5 ears corn, husked and halved
2 lbs. uncooked large shrimp,
   cleaned
Garnish: cocktail sauce, melted
   butter, lemon wedges

Combine water and seasoning in
a large pot; bring to a boil. Add
potatoes and boil, covered, for
15 minutes. Add sausage and
continue to boil for 5 minutes. Add
corn; boil for another 5 minutes.
Add shrimp and boil until shrimp
are pink, about 4 minutes. Drain
and transfer mixture to a large
serving bowl. Garnish as desired.
Serves 6 to 8.

Tanya Schroeder
Cincinnati, OH

This meal is so much fun...
how often do you get to eat
your whole meal with your
hands? Kids love it, adults
love it, and it's a great
summer party idea!

Slowly Simmered
Chicken-Rice Skillet

2 T. oil
4 boneless, skinless chicken
   breasts, cut into bite-size
   pieces
1/2 t. salt
1 t. pepper
1 onion, diced
2 cubes chicken bouillon
2 c. boiling water
1 c. long-cooking rice, uncooked
1 t. lemon zest
1/2 t. dried marjoram
10-oz. pkg. frozen peas

Heat oil in a large skillet over
medium heat. Season chicken with
salt and pepper. Cook chicken in oil
until golden on all sides. Add onion
and sauté for 5 minutes, or until
golden. Add bouillon, water and
rice. Reduce heat to low. Cover and
cook, stirring occasionally, for
25 minutes, or until rice is tender.
Sprinkle lemon zest and marjoram
over chicken mixture. Add peas;
cover and cook over low heat for
10 minutes, or until peas are tender.
Serves 4.

Connie Seago
Sinton, TX

This was one of my mother's
tried & true recipes. She has
been gone for many years, but
my family still loves this
tasty meal...and I love how
simple it is to make.

Slowly Simmered
Dijon Beef Stew

1-1/2 lbs. stew beef cubes
1/4 c. all-purpose flour
2 T. oil
salt and pepper to taste
2 14-1/2 oz. cans diced tomatoes
   with garlic and onion
14-1/2 oz. can beef broth
4 carrots, peeled and cut into
   bite-size pieces
2 potatoes, peeled and cut into
   bite-size pieces
3/4 t. dried thyme
2 T. Dijon mustard

Combine beef and flour in a large
plastic zipping bag; toss to coat
evenly. Add oil to a stockpot over
medium-high heat. Brown beef;
sprinkle with salt and pepper. Add
tomatoes with juice and remaining
ingredients except mustard. Bring
to a boil; reduce heat. Cover and
simmer for one hour, or until
beef is tender. Stir in mustard.
Serves 6 to 8.

Amy Butcher
Columbus, GA

A loaf of crusty French
bread, a salad of mixed
greens and steaming bowls
of this stew...aah. What
could be any better?

Black-Eyed Peas & Potato Skillet

1/3 c. dried black-eyed peas
1-1/2 c. new redskin potatoes,
    halved
1 T. olive oil
1 red onion, diced
1 T. fresh rosemary, chopped
2 T. fresh dill, chopped
1/4 t. salt
2 eggs
Garnish: additional chopped
    fresh dill

Fill a large saucepan with water;
bring to a boil. Add peas and cook
until almost tender, about 15 to
18 minutes. Add potatoes and cook
another 5 to 6 minutes, until
potatoes and peas are tender. Drain
and set aside. Heat oil in a large
skillet over medium heat. Add onion
and cook until translucent, about
4 to 5 minutes. Stir in potatoes, peas
and seasonings. Cook until potatoes
are golden. Make 2 wells in potato
mixture and crack one egg into each
well. Cover and cook until eggs reach
desired doneness. Remove from heat
and sprinkle with dill. Serves 2.

Suzanne Rutan
Auburn, NY

Nothing beats the taste of
freshly snipped dill from
your herb garden...so zesty
and bright! I love the taste
of it, so I try to put it
on everything I can.

Slowly Simmered
Beef Chow Fun

1/2 c. sherry or beef broth
4 t. black bean-garlic sauce
1 T. soy sauce
2 t. light brown sugar, packed
2 t. cornstarch
4 t. oil, divided
1 t. fresh ginger, peeled and
    minced
12-oz. pkg. frozen stir-fry
    vegetables
1/2 c. water, divided
8-oz. pkg. wide rice noodles,
    cooked
8-oz. sirloin beef steak, thinly
    sliced

In a bowl, combine sherry or broth, sauces, brown sugar and cornstarch; set aside. Heat 2 teaspoons oil in a skillet over medium heat. Cook ginger for 30 seconds. Add vegetables and 1/4 cup water; cover and cook, stirring occasionally, until vegetables are tender, about 3 minutes. Combine vegetables and cooked noodles in a bowl; set aside. Heat remaining oil in the same skillet over medium-high heat. Add steak; cook and stir until browned. Stir in sauce mixture; cook until thickened. Return noodle mixture to pan with remaining 1/4 cup water. Cook and stir until evenly coated and warmed through. Serves 4.

Joellen Jubara
Uniontown, OH

This homemade version of a take-out classic is sure to tingle your taste buds. Look for wide rice noodles in the Asian section of your grocery store or at a Chinese market.

Chicken & Apple Wild Rice Soup

2 T. olive oil
2 carrots, peeled and chopped
1 onion, chopped
3 stalks celery, chopped
4 qts. chicken broth
4 boneless, skinless chicken
   breasts, cooked and shredded
1/3 c. wild rice, uncooked
2 t. dried tarragon
1 T. fresh parsley, chopped
salt and pepper to taste
3 Granny Smith apples, peeled,
   cored and chopped

Heat oil in a stockpot over medium heat. Sauté vegetables until tender, about 10 minutes. Add remaining ingredients except apples. Reduce heat to medium-low; cover and simmer for 45 minutes. Add apples and simmer for an additional 40 minutes, or until apples are tender and rice is cooked. Serves 8 to 10.

Tyson Ann Trecannelli
Gettysburg, PA

This is a simple, hearty and delicious soup...so fragrant and sure to call everyone to the table. A perfect dish for fall get-togethers when apples are plentiful.

Skillet Bowtie Lasagna

1 lb. ground beef
1 onion, chopped
1 clove garlic, chopped
14-1/2 oz. can diced tomatoes
1-1/2 c. water
6-oz. can tomato paste
1 T. dried parsley
2 t. dried oregano
1 t. salt
2-1/2 c. bowtie pasta, uncooked
3/4 c. small-curd cottage cheese
1/4 c. grated Parmesan cheese

In a large skillet over medium heat, brown beef, onion and garlic; drain. Add tomatoes with juice, water, tomato paste and seasonings; mix well. Stir in pasta; bring to a boil. Reduce heat, cover and simmer for 20 to 25 minutes, until pasta is tender, stirring once. Combine cheeses; drop by rounded tablespoonfuls onto pasta mixture. Cover and cook for 5 minutes. Serves 4.

61

Trisha Donley
Pinedale, WY

This is one of my favorite go-to meals. I love to serve it with a fresh green salad and slices of warm, buttered Italian bread.

Slowly Simmered
Aunt Annie's Chicken Paprika

2 to 3 c. all-purpose flour
1 t. salt
1/4 t. pepper
4 lbs. chicken
oil for frying
3 onions, sliced
1 clove garlic, chopped
6 carrots, peeled and sliced
2 T. Hungarian paprika
2 c. water
3 cubes chicken bouillon
cooked spaetzle or egg noodles

Mix flour, salt and pepper in a plastic zipping bag. Add chicken pieces, 2 at a time, and toss to coat. Heat 2 tablespoons oil in a Dutch oven over medium-high heat. Sauté onions and garlic until tender; remove from pan and set aside. Add additional oil to about 1/2-inch deep. Add chicken to oil and cook, turning once, until golden on both sides; drain. Remove chicken to a plate and keep warm. Stir in remaining ingredients except spaetzle or noodles. Bring to a boil; return chicken to Dutch oven. Simmer, covered, for one hour over low heat, or until chicken juices run clear. Serve with spaetzle or noodles. Serves 8.

Sandra Lee Smith
Quartz Hill, CA

My Aunt Annie used to cook for several restaurants and cafes...this was one of her best dishes. We made sure to include it in the family cookbook we put together!

Slowly Simmered
Fajitas with Grilled Vegetables

1 lb. boneless beef sirloin,
　　thinly sliced
3/4 c. salsa
2 T. olive oil
2 T. lime juice
Optional: 2 T. tequila
2 cloves garlic, minced
1 red pepper, sliced
1 yellow pepper, sliced
4 slices red onion
1 zucchini, halved and sliced
1 yellow squash, halved and sliced
8 7-inch flour tortillas, warmed
1 c. shredded Mexican-blend
　　cheese

In a large bowl, combine beef, salsa, oil, lime juice, tequila if using, garlic and vegetables; stir to coat well. Cover and refrigerate for least 2 hours. Remove beef and vegetables; reserve marinade. Place beef and vegetables on a grill pan over medium-high heat. Cook for 8 to 10 minutes, until beef is no longer pink and vegetables are tender. Divide beef and vegetables evenly among tortillas. Place reserved marinade in a saucepan over high heat; bring to a boil. Boil marinade for 8 minutes; drizzle over fajitas. Top fajitas with cheese and roll up. Serves 4.

Carol Simmons
Delaware, OH

So yummy! You can substitute your favorite vegetables if you like...just use whatever you have in your garden. The possibilities are endless.

Famous Corn Chip Pie ▶

4 slices bacon, cut into 1-inch
  pieces
2 lbs. ground beef chuck
1 onion, diced
3 cloves garlic, minced
2 t. salt
1/4 c. chili powder, or to taste
1 t. ground cumin
15-oz. can tomato sauce
6-oz. can tomato paste
3/4 c. water
14-oz. pkg. corn chips
8-oz. pkg. shredded sharp
  Cheddar or Monterey Jack
  cheese
Garnish: finely diced red onion,
  diced jalapeño peppers

In a large skillet over medium heat, cook bacon until crisp. Crumble bacon, remove to a plate and set aside, reserving drippings in skillet. Brown beef, onion and garlic in skillet; drain. Stir in seasonings. Add tomato sauce, tomato paste and water to beef mixture. Simmer, stirring occasionally, for 10 to 20 minutes, until thickened. To serve, place a handful of chips in individual bowls. Spoon beef mixture and bacon over chips; sprinkle with cheese. Garnish with onion and jalapeño. Serves 6 to 8.

Tiffani Schulte
Wyandotte, MI
I still remember the amazing
lunch counter at Woolworth's
dimestore. One of their
best-known entrees was their
Corn Chip Pie...a favorite
I've recreated!

Slowly Simmered

Creamy Pumpkin Soup

2 T. oil
1 lb. beef short ribs
4 c. water
3 c. pumpkin, peeled and
    chopped
1 baking potato, peeled and
    cubed
1 carrot, peeled and chopped
1 onion, chopped
salt and pepper to taste

Heat oil in a Dutch oven over medium heat. Brown ribs in oil; drain. Stir in water and bring to a boil. Reduce heat and simmer, covered, one hour. Remove short ribs from Dutch oven, cut off meat and shred; set aside. Stir remaining ingredients into Dutch oven. Simmer, covered, for 45 minutes. Pour half the soup into a blender and process until smooth. Repeat with remaining soup. Stir in reserved beef. Return to Dutch oven and heat through before serving. Serves 6.

Penny Sherman
Ava, MO
This soup is a wonderful way to use up some leftover pumpkin. And for dessert, serve up big slices of pumpkin pie with generous dollops of whipped cream!

Quick Coq au Vin

1/4 c. all-purpose flour
salt and pepper to taste
1 lb. chicken breasts
1/4 c. water
2 T. olive oil, divided
1-1/2 c. sliced mushrooms
2 carrots, peeled and sliced
1 t. dried rosemary
14-oz. can chicken broth
1/2 c. red wine or grape juice
1 T. tomato paste

Combine flour, salt and pepper in a bowl. In a separate bowl, whisk together water and 2 tablespoons flour mixture; set aside. Toss chicken in remaining flour mixture. Heat one tablespoon oil in a skillet over medium heat. Cook chicken until golden on both sides, about 10 minutes. Remove chicken and keep warm. Add remaining oil to pan. Cook vegetables and rosemary until vegetables are softened. Add broth, wine or juice and tomato paste; bring to a simmer. Return chicken to skillet; cover and simmer until cooked through. Transfer chicken and vegetables to a serving plate. Increase heat to medium-high. Stir water mixture into skillet; cook until thickened. Top chicken mixture with sauce and parsley. Serves 4.

Regina Vining
Warwick, RI

A classic French dish simplified for busy cooks. Chicken and vegetables in a savory sauce sprinkled with parsley...what could be more comforting?

Slowly Simmered
Anita's Onion Steaks

15-oz. can beef broth
Optional: 1/2 c. red wine
1.35-oz. pkg. onion soup mix
1 onion, thinly sliced
4 beef cube steaks
pepper to taste
10-3/4 oz. can cream of onion
   soup

In a skillet over medium heat,
combine broth, wine, if using,
and soup mix; mix well. Add onion
and steaks; sprinkle with pepper to
taste. Reduce heat to low; cover and
simmer for 30 minutes. Turn steaks
over; cover and simmer for an
additional 30 minutes. Remove
steaks to a plate; stir soup into
mixture in skillet. Return steaks to
skillet, being sure to coat each steak
with gravy. Cover and simmer over
low heat for 15 minutes. Serves 4.

Anita Mullins
Eldridge, MO
A simply delicious way to fix
budget-friendly cube steaks!
Serve them with mashed
potatoes, cooked egg noodles
or rice, with the gravy from
the skillet ladled over all.

Slowly Simmered
Spinach & Provolone-Stuffed Chicken

1 lb. boneless, skinless chicken
   breasts
1/4 t. pepper
4 thin slices prosciutto ham
10-oz. pkg. frozen chopped
   spinach, thawed and drained
1/4 c. grated Parmesan cheese
2 slices provolone cheese, halved
1 T. olive oil
14-1/2 oz. can low-sodium
   chicken broth

Pound chicken flat; sprinkle with pepper. Place one slice of prosciutto on top of each chicken breast. Spread spinach evenly over prosciutto; sprinkle with Parmesan cheese. Top each chicken breast with a slice of provolone cheese and roll up, starting at tapered end. Secure each roll with a toothpick. Heat oil in a skillet over medium-high heat. Cook rolls in oil, turning once, until golden on both sides, about 8 minutes. Add broth and bring to a boil. Reduce heat to medium-low; cover and simmer for 10 minutes, or until chicken is no longer pink in the center. Transfer rolls to a serving plate; keep warm. Increase heat to high; cook until liquid in skillet is thickened. Drizzle sauce over rolls. Serves 4.

Kendall Hale
Lynn, MA

This dish looks as if it took all day to make, but it really doesn't take long at all. Serve with some fresh asparagus and a salad for a beautiful meal.

Delicious Pot Roast

4-lb. boneless beef chuck roast
2 cloves garlic, sliced
1/2 t. salt
1/2 t. pepper
1/4 c. all-purpose flour
1/3 c. olive oil
1 onion, sliced
1 c. red wine or beef broth
8-oz. can tomato sauce
1 T. brown sugar, packed
1 t. dried oregano
1 t. prepared horseradish
1 t. mustard
1 bay leaf
8 new red potatoes
6 carrots, peeled and quartered
4 stalks celery, sliced

Cut small slits in the top of roast; insert a slice of garlic into each slit. Season with salt and pepper. Place flour in a bowl; dredge roast in flour. Heat oil in a Dutch oven over medium heat. Brown roast on both sides in oil. Add onion and wine or broth. Combine tomato sauce, sugar and seasonings in a bowl; pour over roast. Bring to a boil; reduce heat, cover and simmer for 1-1/2 hours. Add remaining ingredients. Cover and cook for one hour. Discard bay leaf. Serve with sauce from Dutch oven over top. Serves 8.

Nancy Girard
Chesapeake, VA

Pot roast is always a favorite at our house, and I have many different recipes for fixing it. But this recipe is the one that's most requested.

Slowly Simmered
Fluffy Chicken & Dumplings

1 to 2 T. oil
1 c. celery, chopped
1 c. carrots, peeled and sliced
1 T. onion, chopped
49-oz. can chicken broth
10-3/4 oz. can cream of chicken
  soup
1/8 t. pepper
2 c. cooked chicken, cubed
1-2/3 c. biscuit baking mix
2/3 c. milk

Heat oil in a Dutch oven over medium-high heat. Sauté celery, carrots and onion in oil for about 7 minutes, until crisp-tender. Add broth, soup and pepper; bring to a boil. Reduce heat to low; stir in chicken and bring to a simmer. In a separate bowl, stir together baking mix and milk. Drop batter by tablespoonfuls into simmering broth. Cover and cook over low heat for 15 minutes without lifting lid. Serves 6.

Angela Lengacher
Montgomery, IN

This is a wonderful way to warm up on a chilly night! Soft, fluffy dumplings in a warm and & hearty mixture of chicken and vegetables... pure comfort food.

Slowly Simmered
Picture-Perfect Paella

3 lbs. chicken
2 onions, quartered
1 stalk celery, sliced
2 carrots, peeled and sliced
salt and pepper to taste
6 c. water
2 c. long-cooking rice, uncooked
2 cloves garlic, crushed
1/4 c. oil
1 c. peas
1/4 c. diced pimentos, drained
1/2 t. dried oregano
1/8 t. saffron or turmeric
1 lb. uncooked large shrimp,
   peeled and cleaned
12 uncooked clams in shells

In a large skillet over medium heat, combine chicken pieces, onions, celery, carrots, salt, pepper and water. Bring to a boil; reduce heat, cover and simmer for one hour. Remove vegetables and chicken, reserving 6 cups broth. Dice chicken and set meat aside, discarding bones. In the same skillet over medium heat, cook and stir rice and garlic in oil until golden. Add reserved chicken, reserved broth, peas, pimentos, oregano and saffron or turmeric. Cover and cook over low heat for 15 minutes. Add shrimp and clams; cover and cook for another 10 minutes, or until shrimp are pink and clams have opened. Serves 8.

Jo Ann
This classic Spanish dish is not only beautiful to look at, it's also amazingly delicious. It takes a little time to prepare, but it's so worth it.

Slowly Simmered
Mom's Cola Chicken

1 to 2 T. oil
1-1/2 lbs. boneless, skinless
   chicken breasts
salt and pepper to taste
20-oz. bottle cola, divided
1 to 2 c. catsup, divided

Heat oil in a large skillet over
medium heat. Add chicken to oil;
sprinkle with salt and pepper and
brown on both sides. Pour enough
cola into skillet to cover chicken.
Slowly add enough catsup to skillet
until mixture reaches desired
thicknesss. Cover and cook over
medium heat for about 45 minutes,
adding remaining cola and catsup,
a little at a time, every 10 to
15 minutes, until chicken juices
run clear. Serves 4.

Carla Slajchert
St. Petersburg, FL

Growing up, we knew Mom
would be making this
delicious, tender chicken
whenever we saw her get
out the electric skillet.

Slowly Simmered

Rosemary Chicken & Tomatoes

1 T. oil
2 lbs. skinless chicken thighs
2/3 c. chicken broth
1/4 c. white wine or chicken
  broth
2 cloves garlic, minced
salt and pepper to taste
6 plum tomatoes, chopped
2 green peppers, cut into strips
1-1/2 c. sliced mushrooms
2 T. cornstarch
2 T. cold water
2 t. fresh rosemary, snipped
cooked egg noodles or rice

Heat oil in a skillet over medium heat. Sauté chicken in oil until golden, about 5 minutes; drain. Add broth, wine or broth, garlic, salt and pepper; bring to a boil. Reduce heat; cover and simmer for 20 minutes. Add tomatoes, peppers and mushrooms. Simmer, covered, for 15 minutes, or until chicken is cooked through. Transfer chicken to a serving dish and keep warm. In a small bowl, combine cornstarch, water and rosemary; stir into vegetable mixture. Cook and stir until thickened and bubbly. Serve chicken over noodles or rice; spoon sauce over chicken. Serves 5.

Vickie

Tender, slow-simmered chicken at its best...I like to use the plum tomatoes and rosemary from my garden. It doesn't get any fresher than that!

Super-Simple Swiss Steak

1 lb. beef round steak, sliced
   into 6 pieces
1 t. garlic powder
salt and pepper to taste
1/4 c. all-purpose flour
1/3 c. oil
2 cloves garlic, crushed
1 onion, sliced
1 green pepper, sliced
14-1/2 oz. can diced tomatoes
1-1/4 c. water

Season steak on all sides with garlic powder, salt and pepper. Place flour in a shallow bowl; dredge steak in flour until evenly coated. Heat oil in a Dutch oven over medium heat. Cook steak until browned on all sides. Reduce heat to low; add remaining ingredients. Cook, covered, for 1-1/2 hours, or until steak is tender and cooked through, adding more water to cover steak if needed. Serves 6.

Kathy Harris
Valley Center, KS
This is one of the easiest ways to make Swiss Steak... and it's so delicious.

Slowly Simmered
Pork Chops Olé

2 T. oil
4 pork chops
2 T. butter
6.8-oz. pkg. Spanish-flavored
   rice vermicelli mix
14-1/2 oz. can Mexican-style
   stewed tomatoes
1-1/2 c. water
Garnish: sour cream, chopped
   fresh cilantro

Heat oil in a large skillet over medium heat. Cook pork chops in oil until browned on both sides, about 6 minutes; remove from skillet and keep warm. Melt butter in same skillet; add rice mix to butter. Cook and stir until rice mix is lightly golden. Stir in tomatoes with juice and water. Add pork chops to skillet and bring to a boil. Reduce heat to low; cover and cook for 20 to 30 minutes, until liquid is absorbed and pork chops are no longer pink in the center. Garnish with sour cream and cilantro. Serves 4.

Julie De Fusco
Las Vegas, NV

This was one of my favorite dishes to make when I was just learning to cook...it's so easy and so tasty. Make it spicier by adding a little chopped jalapeño.

Slowly Simmered
Pasta Trapanese

1 onion, chopped
2 cloves garlic, pressed
1/4 c. olive oil
28-oz. can whole Italian plum
   tomatoes, crushed
5 to 6 T. fresh basil, chopped
salt and pepper to taste
1/4 c. slivered almonds, toasted
12-oz. pkg. penne pasta, cooked
Garnish: grated Parmesan cheese

In a skillet over medium heat, sauté onion and garlic in oil. Add tomatoes with juice, basil, salt and pepper. Reduce heat and simmer, uncovered, for 30 minutes. Stir in almonds. Serve sauce over cooked pasta, garnished with Parmesan cheese. Serves 4.

Claudia Passaro
Chester, NJ

This is a Sicilian recipe that was given to me by my mother. We chose this delectable sauce for the pasta course at our wedding dinner...it was a huge hit!

Slowly Simmered
Classic Corned Beef & Cabbage

2 to 3 onions, chopped
1-1/4 lbs. baby carrots
3-lb. corned beef brisket with
  seasoning packet
1/2 c. malt vinegar
Optional: 1/4 c. Irish stout
1-1/4 lbs. redskin potatoes
1 to 1-1/2 heads cabbage, cut into
  serving-size wedges
Garnish: coarse-grain mustard,
  Dijon mustard

Place onions, carrots, corned beef,
seasoning packet, vinegar and stout,
if using, in a large stockpot. Add
enough water to just cover beef.
Cover and bring to a boil. Reduce
heat to medium-low and simmer for
2-1/2 to 3 hours, until beef is tender.
Add potatoes and cabbage. Increase
heat to high; cover and simmer for
8 to 10 minutes. Reduce heat to
medium and simmer an additional
15 minutes, or until potatoes are
tender. Remove vegetables to a
serving dish; place beef on a cutting
board. Let rest 3 minutes; slice
against the grain. Serve with
vegetables and mustards.
Serves 6 to 8.

Heidi McInnish
Chula Vista, CA

A St. Patrick's Day
tradition...but much too
delicious to enjoy only
once a year!

Tempting Teriyaki Chicken

2/3 c. soy sauce
1/3 c. sugar
1/4 t. ground ginger
1/8 t. garlic powder
4 to 5 boneless, skinless chicken
    breasts
cooked rice
Garnish: sliced green onions,
    sesame seeds

In a large skillet over medium heat, whisk together soy sauce, sugar, ginger and garlic powder. When heated through, add chicken. Cover and simmer, basting chicken occasionally with sauce, for about 30 minutes, until chicken is no longer pink in the center. Uncover and cook an additional 10 minutes, or until sauce thickens. Serve with rice; garnish with green onions and sesame seeds. Serves 4 to 6.

Amy Holt
Enterprise, UT
I have to triple this recipe
when I make it for my
family...they absolutely
love it.

Slowly Simmered
Chicken Cranberry Ruby

1/3 c. all-purpose flour
1 t. salt
2 lbs. chicken
1/4 c. butter
1-1/2 c. fresh cranberries
3/4 c. sugar
1/4 c. onion, chopped
1 t. orange zest
3/4 c. orange juice
1/4 t. cinnamon
1/4 t. ground ginger

Combine flour and salt in a large plastic zipping bag. Working in batches, add chicken pieces to flour mixture and shake to coat well. Melt butter in a large skillet over medium heat. Cook chicken, turning once, until golden on all sides, about 10 minutes. Meanwhile, combine remaining ingredients in saucepan over medium-high heat; bring to a boil. Pour cranberry mixture over chicken in skillet. Reduce heat to low; cover and cook for 35 to 40 minutes, until chicken is no longer pink in the center and sauce has thickened. Serves 4 to 6.

Nancy Ziebell
Onalaska, WI

The sweet cranberry coating on this chicken always reminds me of fall. At first I was skeptical of this recipe, but it's so tasty that now I make it year 'round!

Slowly Simmered
Tortilla Stew

2 15-1/2 oz. cans hominy
2 15-1/2 oz. cans chili beans
2 14-1/2 oz. cans Mexican-style
   stewed tomatoes
2 11-oz. cans sweet corn &
   diced peppers
2 10-oz. cans diced tomatoes
   with green chiles
2 10-oz. cans chicken, drained
2 1-oz. pkgs. ranch salad
   dressing mix
1/2 onion, chopped
salt and pepper to taste
tortilla chips
Garnish: shredded cheese,
   sour cream, guacamole

Stir together undrained vegetables
and all ingredients except chips and
garnish in a large stockpot. Simmer
over medium heat for 30 minutes.
Place a handful of chips into
individual serving bowls; spoon stew
over chips. Garnish as desired.
Serves 8 to 10.

Donna Cannon
Tulsa, OK

My family absolutely loves
this stew, especially in cold
weather. It's ready in less
than 40 minutes...perfect
for busy schedules!

Slowly Simmered
Mom's Spaghetti & Meatballs

2 8-oz. cans tomato sauce
1/2 t. garlic powder
1/2 t. dried oregano
1/2 t. dried basil
16-oz. pkg. spaghetti, cooked

In a large skillet over medium-low heat, combine tomato sauce and seasonings. Bring to a simmer. Meanwhile, make Meatballs. Add uncooked meatballs to sauce. Simmer over medium-low heat for about 30 minutes, turning occasionally, until meatballs are no longer pink in the center. Serve sauce and meatballs over spaghetti. Serves 4 to 6.

Meatballs:

1 lb. lean ground beef
1/2 c. shredded Cheddar cheese
2 eggs, beaten
1 slice white bread, crumbled
1/2 t. garlic salt

Combine all ingredients in a large bowl; mix well. Form into 2-inch balls.

Elaine Lucas
Runge, TX

This started out as my mom's recipe. I've since made it my own over the years, and it's become a family favorite.

Slowly Simmered
Chocolate-Hazelnut Skillet Bars

1-1/4 c. all-purpose flour
1/4 t. baking powder
1/2 t. baking soda
1/2 t. salt
1/2 c. butter
1 c. dark brown sugar, packed
1 egg, beaten
1-1/2 t. vanilla extract
1 t. espresso powder
3/4 c. dark baking chocolate,
    chopped
1/2 c. hazelnuts, chopped

In a bowl, combine flour, baking powder, baking soda and salt; set aside. Melt butter in a large cast-iron skillet over medium heat. Add brown sugar and whisk until sugar is dissolved, about one minute. Slowly pour butter mixture into flour mixture. Add egg, vanilla and espresso powder to flour mixture; stir until combined. Fold in remaining ingredients. Spoon dough into skillet; bake at 350 degrees for 20 to 25 minutes, until golden on top and a toothpick tests clean. Let stand 30 minutes; slice into wedges to serve. Serves 8.

Cheri Maxwell
Gulf Breeze, FL

These blondie-like bars are too good to pass up. If you aren't a fan of hazelnuts, pecans, almonds or even peanuts would be just as tasty!

Slowly Simmered
Coconutty Nanaimo Bars

1 c. butter, divided
1/4 c. sugar
5 T. baking cocoa
1 egg, beaten
1-3/4 c. graham cracker crumbs
1 c. sweetened flaked coconut
1/4 c. milk
1/4 c. instant vanilla pudding mix
2 c. powdered sugar
1/2 c. semi-sweet chocolate chips, melted
1/2 c. sweetened flaked coconut, toasted

In a saucepan over low heat, combine 1/2 cup butter, sugar and cocoa; cook and stir until butter melts. Remove from heat and slowly whisk in egg. Return to heat and cook until thickened. Stir in graham cracker crumbs and untoasted coconut. Remove from heat and let cool slightly; press into a lightly greased 8"x8" baking pan and set aside. In a bowl, beat together remaining butter, milk, pudding mix and powdered sugar; spread over graham cracker mixture. Spread melted chocolate chips on top; sprinkle with toasted coconut. Refrigerate for at least one hour before serving. Slice into bars. Serves 8.

**Lisa Teeter
Hollsopple, PA**

If you have a chocolate craving or a sweet tooth, this is a quick and simple recipe for you. Even better...you don't have to bake them!

Speedy Chicken Gumbo

3 T. oil
1/3 c. all-purpose flour
1 onion, chopped
2 red peppers, chopped
3 cloves garlic, minced
1 t. dried oregano
salt and pepper to taste
4 c. water
10-oz. pkg. frozen cut okra,
   thawed
8-oz. smoked andouille sausage,
   halved lengthwise and sliced
   1-inch thick
1 deli roast chicken, boned
   and shredded

In a large stockpot, heat oil over medium heat. Add flour; cook for 5 to 7 minutes, whisking constantly, until golden. Stir in onion, red peppers, garlic and oregano. Season with salt and pepper. Cook, stirring constantly, until vegetables are crisp-tender, about 10 to 12 minutes. Add water; stir in okra and sausage. Bring to a boil. Stir in shredded chicken and warm through. Serves 6.

Kathy Harris
Valley Center, KS
This gumbo is a staple at our house because it can be made quickly and transported easily. It's delicious served over cornbread.

Taco in a Pan ▶

1 lb. ground beef
1/2 c. onion, chopped
1/2 c. green pepper, chopped
2 c. water
1-1/4 oz. pkg. taco seasoning mix
1-1/2 c. instant rice, uncooked
1 c. salsa, or to taste
1 c. shredded Colby Jack cheese
1 tomato, chopped
Optional: 1 c. sliced black olives
Garnish: crushed nacho-flavored
   tortilla chips

Brown beef, onion and green
pepper in a skillet over medium
heat; drain. Stir water and taco
seasoning into beef mixture. Bring
to a boil; stir in rice. Cover and
cook for 3 to 5 minutes, until rice
is tender. Sprinkle salsa and cheese
over all. Remove from heat; cover
and let stand until cheese melts. Top
with tomato and olives, if desired.
Garnish with chips. Serves 4 to 6.

Peggy Sanders
Adair, IA
This recipe was originally
given to me by my mother.
It's a family favorite that's
asked for time & time again.
I have since passed it on
to my sons.

Creamy White Chili

1 T. oil
1 lb. boneless, skinless chicken
   breast, cubed
1 onion, chopped
14-oz. can chicken broth
2 15-1/2 oz. cans Great
   Northern beans, drained
   and rinsed
2 4-oz. cans chopped green
   chiles
1-1/2 t. garlic powder
1 t. salt
1 t. ground cumin
1/2 t. dried oregano
8-oz. container sour cream
1/2 pt. whipping cream
Garnish: crushed corn chips,
   shredded Monterey Jack cheese

Heat oil in a large skillet over medium heat; add chicken and onion. Sauté until chicken is cooked through; set aside. Combine broth, beans, chiles and seasonings in a large soup pot over medium-high heat; bring to a boil. Add chicken mixture; reduce heat and simmer for 30 minutes. Add sour cream and whipping cream; mix well. Garnish individual servings with chips and cheese. Serves 8.

Janelle Dixon
Fernley, NV

This chili has such a fabulous flavor with its blend of green chiles, cumin, sour cream and chicken... a perfect change from the same ol' chili.

Maryland Crab Cakes

Karen Thomas
Princess Anne, MD

A true Maryland summer treat...top with a dollop of mayonnaise if you like. Crab cakes make scrumptious sandwiches or salad toppings too.

1 lb. crabmeat, flaked
3 T. mayonnaise
1 c. saltine crackers, crushed
1 t. seafood seasoning or pepper
1 t. mustard
2 t. Worcestershire sauce
1 egg, beaten
oil for frying

Mix together all ingredients except oil; form into 8 patties. Heat 1/8 inch of oil in a skillet over medium heat. Fry patties in oil until golden on both sides. Drain on paper towels. Serves 8.

87

Grilled Sausage & Veggie Packs

1 lb. Kielbasa sausage, cut into
   bite-size pieces
4 to 5 redskin potatoes, cut into
   bite-size cubes
1 red onion, thinly sliced
1 zucchini, cut into 1-inch cubes
16-oz. pkg. baby carrots
1 yellow squash, cut into 1-inch
   cubes
butter or olive oil to taste
salt, pepper, minced garlic,
   dried parsley and Italian
   seasoning to taste

Arrange sausage and vegetables on a
large piece of heavy-duty aluminum
foil coated with non-stick vegetable
spray. Dot with butter or drizzle with
oil. Season as desired. Seal edges of
foil tightly to create a packet. Place
on a grill pan over medium heat;
cook for about one hour, until
vegetables are tender. Serves 6.

Cindy Edmondson
Red Creek, NY
Our family loves vegetables
roasted in a foil pack on
the grill, so I created
this main-dish meal we
all enjoy.

Hunting Cabin Chili

2 to 3 lbs. ground beef
1 onion, chopped
1 green pepper, chopped
16-oz. jar salsa
30-oz. can light red kidney
   beans, drained
3 15-1/2 oz. cans dark red
   kidney beans, drained
28-oz. can whole tomatoes
1/8 t. hot pepper sauce
salt to taste

Brown beef in a large soup pot over
medium heat; drain. Add remaining
ingredients to pot. If needed, add
enough water to just cover ingredients.
Bring to a boil. Reduce to low; cover
and simmer for 2 to 3 hours, until
thickened. Serves 8 to 10.

89

Wendy West Hickey
Wexford, PA

This spicy chili goes great
with large buttered squares
of cornbread...top bowls with
crushed corn chips and a
sprinkling of cheese.

New England Fish Chowder

1 T. oil
1/2 c. onion, chopped
2-1/2 c. potatoes, peeled
   and diced
1-1/2 c. boiling water
salt and pepper to taste
1 lb. frozen cod or haddock
   fillets, thawed and cut into
   large chunks
2 c. milk
1 T. butter

Heat oil in a large saucepan over medium heat. Add onion and sauté until tender. Add potatoes, water, salt and pepper. Reduce heat; cover and simmer for 15 to 20 minutes, until potatoes are tender. Add fish; simmer until fish flakes easily with a fork, about 5 minutes. Just before serving, add milk and butter; stir well and heat through. Makes 6 servings.

Lynda Robson
Boston, MA

Such a hearty and flavorful chowder. Garnish with oyster crackers and chopped fresh green onion for a perfect treat.

Tomato & Chicken Penne ▶

1/4 c. olive oil
1 t. garlic, chopped
28-oz. can diced tomatoes, drained
1/2 c. fresh basil, chopped
2 lbs. boneless, skinless chicken breasts, cooked and cubed
16-oz. pkg. penne pasta, cooked
8-oz. pkg. shredded mozzarella cheese
salt and pepper to taste

Heat oil in a skillet over medium heat. Add garlic; sauté for one minute. Stir in tomatoes and basil; continue cooking for 2 minutes. Add chicken to skillet. Sauté for about 5 minutes, until heated through. Transfer chicken mixture to a large serving bowl; toss with pasta and cheese. Season with salt and pepper. Makes 6 to 8 servings.

Stefani St. Pierre
South Dennis, MA

This is a wonderfully hearty dish that's easy to prepare...just stir together everything in one pot and you've got a bright, flavorful dinner in no time.

Sausage Patties & Marinara Sauce

3 T. olive oil
3/4 c. onion, chopped
1 clove garlic, minced
14-1/2 oz. can diced tomatoes
15-oz. can tomato sauce
12-oz. can tomato paste
2 c. water
1 t. sugar
1 t. salt
1/2 t. pepper
1-1/2 t. dried oregano
1 bay leaf
3 T. grated Romano cheese
1 lb. ground hot Italian pork
    sausage, formed into 8 patties
16-oz. pkg. spaghetti pasta,
    cooked
Garnish: grated Parmesan cheese

Heat oil in a Dutch oven over
medium heat. Sauté onion and garlic
until tender. Stir in tomatoes with
juice, tomato sauce, tomato paste,
water, sugar and seasonings. Reduce
heat to medium-low and simmer for
30 minutes. Discard bay leaf; stir in
Romano cheese. Cover and cook for
30 minutes. Brown sausage patties
in a skillet on both sides until no
longer pink in the middle, about
10 minutes. Divide pasta among
bowls; top with a sausage patty and
sauce. Garnish with cheese. Serves 8.

Nancy Gasko
South Bend, IN

There's a great Italian
restaurant in town that makes
this dish. According to my
husband, theirs is the best
around. So I whipped up this
recipe, which he says is
just as good!

Sunday Meeting Tomato Soup

1/2 c. butter, sliced
1 c. fresh basil, chopped
2 28-oz. cans crushed tomatoes
2 cloves garlic, minced
1 qt. half-and-half
salt and pepper to taste
Garnish: croutons, shredded
   Parmesan cheese

In a large saucepan, melt butter over medium heat. Add basil; sauté for 2 minutes. Add tomatoes with juice and garlic. Reduce heat and simmer for 20 minutes. Remove from heat; let cool slightly. Working in batches, transfer tomato mixture to a blender and purée. Transfer back into saucepan and add half-and-half, mixing well. Reheat soup over medium-low heat; add salt and pepper to taste. Serve topped with croutons and shredded Parmesan cheese. Makes 10 servings.

93

Gretchen Ham
Pine City, NY
Fresh basil really makes this soup special. It's often requested at our church's Sunday soup & sandwich lunches after the services.

Lucky-7 Mac & Cheese

1 c. milk
1/2 c. extra-sharp Cheddar
   cheese, diced
1/2 c. Colby cheese, diced
1/2 c. pasteurized process cheese
   spread, diced
1/2 c. Swiss cheese, diced
1/2 c. provolone cheese, diced
1/2 c. Monterey Jack cheese,
   diced
1/2 c. crumbled blue cheese
16-oz. pkg. elbow macaroni,
   cooked
salt and pepper to taste

In a heavy saucepan, combine milk
and cheeses. Heat over low to
medium heat until melted, stirring
often. Fold in macaroni; season
with salt and pepper. Heat through,
stirring occasionally. Makes 6 to
8 servings.

Tina Vogel
Orlando, FL

Wow! This homestyle favorite
has seven kinds of cheese...
sure to be one of the
cheesiest, tastiest mac &
cheeses you've ever had.

Coconut Mahi-Mahi

3 T. oil
2 T. curry powder
1 onion, finely chopped
1 red pepper, diced
1 t. jalapeño pepper, seeded
 and minced
2 cloves garlic, minced
1 t. fresh thyme, chopped
13.6-oz. can coconut milk
2 lbs. mahi-mahi fillets
2 green onions, thinly sliced
salt and pepper to taste

Heat oil in a large skillet over medium heat. Add curry powder to oil and cook for one minute. Add onion, peppers, garlic and thyme. Cook, stirring occasionally, until vegetables are crisp-tender, about 2 minutes. Stir in coconut milk and bring to a simmer. Add fish and green onions to skillet; cover and cook until fish flakes easily with a fork, about 5 to 7 minutes. Sprinkle with salt and pepper. Serves 6 to 8.

Darrell Lawry
Kissimmee, FL

This spicy, flavorful dish is one of my favorites. It's sure to warm you up from head to toe...if you don't like it too spicy, just omit the jalapeño pepper.

Ham & Potato Skillet Supper

4-1/2 t. butter
3 baking potatoes, peeled and
   thinly sliced
1/2 onion, chopped
1/2 green pepper, chopped
2 c. cooked ham, diced
salt and pepper to taste
3 eggs, lightly beaten
1/2 c. shredded Cheddar cheese

Melt butter in a large skillet over medium heat. Layer half each of the potatoes, onion, green pepper and ham in skillet. Repeat layers; season with salt and pepper. Cover and cook for 10 to 15 minutes, until potatoes are tender. Pour eggs over potato mixture; cover and cook for 3 to 5 minutes, until eggs are almost set. Sprinkle cheese over all. Remove from heat; cover and let stand until cheese is melted. Cut into wedges to serve. Serves 6.

Suzanne Fritz
Hutto, TX

This is a versatile dish that we sometimes eat for breakfast too. It's so good topped with a dash of hot sauce, picante sauce or sour cream.

Bowties, Sausage & Beans

1 T. olive oil
6 hot Italian pork sausage links,
    sliced into thirds
1 tomato, chopped
2 15-oz. cans cannellini beans
10-oz. pkg. fresh spinach
garlic powder and dried basil
    to taste
12-oz. pkg. bowtie pasta, cooked

Heat oil in a Dutch oven over
medium heat. Cook sausage until
browned on all sides and no longer
pink in the center; stir in tomato.
Simmer, stirring occasionally, until
tomato is soft. Stir in beans and
seasonings; heat through. Fold in
spinach. Cover and simmer until
spinach is wilted, about 6 to
8 minutes. Stir in pasta; toss to
mix and heat through. Serves 6.

**Christy Young
North Attleboro, MA**

This is a hearty and
delicious meal anytime...
stellar served with a side
salad and thick slices of
Italian bread.

Grilled Tilapia with Pineapple Salsa

2 c. pineapple, cubed
2 green onions, chopped
1/4 c. green pepper, diced
1/4 c. fresh cilantro, minced
2 T. plus 4 t. lime juice, divided
1/4 t. plus 1/8 t. salt, divided
1/8 t. cayenne pepper
1 T. canola oil
2 lbs. tilapia fillets
1/8 t. pepper

In a small bowl, combine pineapple, onions, green pepper, cilantro, 4 teaspoons lime juice, 1/8 teaspoon salt and cayenne pepper. Mix well and chill until serving time. In a separate small bowl, combine oil and remaining lime juice. Brush over fillets; sprinkle with pepper and remaining salt. Cook fish on a grill pan over medium heat, turning once, for 6 to 8 minutes, until fish flakes easily with a fork. Serve fish topped with pineapple salsa. Serves 6 to 8.

Geneve Rogers
Gillette, WY

When we went to Florida on vacation, I had a dish very similar to this one...it was out-of-this-world good. So when we got home, I just had to try and make it myself.

Southwestern Corn Skillet

1 lb. ground beef
1/2 c. onion, chopped
26-oz. jar pasta sauce
11-oz. can sweet corn &
    diced peppers
1/2 t. salt
8-oz. pkg rotini pasta, cooked
1 c. shredded Cheddar cheese
4 green onions, sliced

Brown beef and onion in a skillet
over medium heat; drain. Stir in
pasta sauce, corn, salt and pasta.
Cook and stir until heated through.
Remove from heat and sprinkle
with cheese. Cover and let stand
until cheese is melted; sprinkle with
green onions. Serve 6.

99

Emma Brown
Ontario, Canada
This is one of the easiest
dishes I make. All the
hearty southwestern flavors
and gooey cheese...definitely
a stick-to-your-ribs meal.

Curried Chicken with Mango

2 T. oil
4 boneless, skinless chicken
 breasts, cooked and cubed
13.6-oz. can coconut milk
1 c. mango, peeled, pitted
 and cubed
2 to 3 T. curry powder
cooked jasmine rice

Heat oil in a large skillet over
medium heat. Cook chicken in oil
until golden and warmed through.
Stir in milk, mango and curry
powder. Simmer for 10 minutes,
stirring occasionally, or until slightly
thickened. Serve over rice.
Serves 4 to 6.

Cecilia Ollivares
Santa Paula, CA
I love dishes that don't take
too long to make, and this
recipe is delicious and
speedy...perfect served with
a side of naan flatbread.

Savory Beans & Tomatoes over Rice

4 to 6 slices bacon, diced
1 onion, diced
1 stalk celery, diced
1 T. garlic, chopped
14-1/2 oz. can diced tomatoes
2 15-1/2 oz. cans cannellini
   beans
hot pepper sauce and red pepper
   flakes to taste
1/8 t. Italian seasoning
2 to 3 T. butter
salt and pepper to taste
cooked rice

In a large skillet over medium heat, cook bacon until crisp. Remove bacon to a plate and keep warm, reserving drippings in pan. Sauté onion and celery in drippings until translucent. Stir in garlic and cook for 2 to 3 minutes. Add tomatoes with juice to onion mixture; bring to a simmer, stirring occasionally. Stir in undrained beans; return to a simmer. Add reserved bacon and remaining ingredients except rice to skillet; heat through. To serve, spoon over rice. Serves 6 to 8.

Jewell Ulrich
Colorado Springs, CO
This delicious meal is just minutes away...packed with flavor and so satisfying!

Mom's Chicken Riggies

2 to 3 T. oil
2 T. garlic, minced
2 boneless, skinless chicken
    breasts, cubed
8-oz. pkg. sliced mushrooms
1 green pepper, diced
26-oz. jar spaghetti sauce
Optional: 1/2 to 1 c. white wine
1 pt. whipping cream
16-oz. pkg. rigatoni pasta,
    cooked

Add oil to a skillet over medium heat; sauté garlic until lightly golden. Add chicken; sauté until lightly golden and no longer pink in the middle. Add mushrooms and green pepper; cook until soft. Reduce heat to low. Pour sauce into a separate saucepan. Add wine, if using, and heat through. Stir in cream in small amounts until sauce becomes orange in color. Add to chicken mixture in skillet; stir to mix. Place cooked pasta in a large serving bowl. Top with sauce mixture and toss to mix. Makes 8 to 10 servings.

Justine Hutchings
New York Mills, NY
I'm from central New York, and "Riggies" is a very popular dish here. My mother taught me how to make this quick & easy recipe.

Beef Porcupine Meatballs

8-oz. pkg. beef-flavored rice
    vermicelli mix
1 lb. ground beef
1 egg, beaten
2-1/2 c. water
cooked egg noodles

In a bowl, combine rice vermicelli mix, beef and egg, reserving seasoning packet from mix. Form mixture into one-inch balls. In a skillet over medium heat, cook meatballs, turning occasionally, until browned on all sides; drain. In a bowl, combine seasoning packet and water; pour over meatballs. Cover and simmer for 30 minutes, or until thickened and meatballs are no longer pink in the center. Serve meatballs and sauce over noodles. Makes 4 to 6 servings.

103

Terri Lock
Carrollton, MO

As a teacher, I need fast homestyle meals to serve to my family of five before I leave for evening school events...this recipe is perfect.

Creamed Chicken on Biscuits

2 T. butter
1/2 c. celery, chopped
1 T. green pepper, chopped
1-1/2 t. onion, chopped
1/4 c. all-purpose flour
1-1/2 c. chicken broth
1/2 c. milk
1-1/2 c. cooked chicken, diced
1/8 t. salt
8-oz. tube refrigerated biscuits,
  baked and split

Melt butter in a large saucepan over medium heat. Cook celery, pepper and onion until tender. Blend in flour; stir in broth and milk. Cook and stir over medium heat until smooth. Add chicken and salt; heat through. Spoon over biscuits to serve. Makes 8 servings.

Kathy Wyers
Cambridge, OH

A fast, tasty way to use up leftover chicken or turkey. This is the perfect comfort food after a long day of apple picking and leaf raking.

Seafood Linguine with a Kick

3 T. butter
3 T. extra-virgin olive oil
8 cloves garlic, pressed
2 shallots, thinly sliced
3 T. red pepper flakes, divided
1/2 lb. uncooked large shrimp,
   peeled and cleaned
1/2 lb. scallops
1/2 lb. imitation crabmeat,
   chopped
2 28-oz. cans petite diced
   tomatoes, drained
3 T. sugar
2 T. fresh basil, thinly sliced
16-oz. pkg. linguine pasta,
   cooked

Combine butter and oil in a large skillet over medium heat. Sauté garlic, shallots and 1-1/2 tablespoons red pepper flakes until tender. Add shrimp and scallops; cook for 5 to 10 minutes, until shrimp are pink. Stir in crabmeat and heat through. Remove seafood to a plate and keep warm. Add tomatoes, sugar and remaining red pepper flakes to skillet. Bring to a boil, stirring occasionally; reduce heat and simmer for 15 minutes. Add basil and seafood to tomato mixture; spoon over pasta. Serves 8.

Lee Beedle
Martinsburg, WV
My husband just loves this dish...and that's saying a lot since he's not much of a pasta person! He likes it so much he requests it at least once a month.

Simple Skillet Peaches

6 c. peaches, peeled, pitted and
  cut into bite-size pieces
1/2 c. sugar
1 T. vanilla extract

Combine peaches and sugar in a
large skillet over medium heat.
Bring to a boil; reduce heat to
medium-low. Simmer until peaches
are soft and mixture has thickened,
about 20 to 25 minutes. Stir in
extract. Serve warm or store in an
airtight container in the refrigerator.
Makes about 6 servings.

Tina Wright
Atlanta, GA
These peaches are delicious
on just about anything you
can think of. Cereal, oatmeal,
ice cream, cobbler...or use
them to top big slices of
angel food cake!

Pineapple Pudding

12-oz. pkg. vanilla wafers,
    divided
1/3 c. sugar
3 T. cornstarch
1/4 t. salt
2-1/2 c. milk
1-1/2 t. vanilla extract
20-oz. can crushed pineapple,
    drained
8-oz. container frozen whipped
    topping, thawed
Garnish: pineapple slices,
    maraschino cherries

Layer wafers in a large glass trifle
bowl until bottom is covered,
reserving 8 to 10 for garnish. In a
saucepan over medium heat, combine
sugar, cornstarch and salt. Stir in
milk. Cook, stirring occasionally,
until mixture thickens. Add vanilla
and cook for 2 to 3 minutes. Once
mixture is thick, fold in crushed
pineapple. Spread pudding mixture
over wafers in bowl; let cool. Top
pudding with whipped topping.
Garnish with pineapple slices,
reserved wafers and cherries.
Serves 6.

Debra Elliott
Birmingham, AL
This pineapple pudding
is my favorite. It's an
easy-to-make, mouthwatering
dessert that will tickle
your taste buds.

INDEX

Beef

Anita's Onion Steaks, 67
Beef & Bean Tostadas, 36
Beef Chow Fun, 59
Beef Porcupine Meatballs, 103
Classic Corned Beef & Cabbage, 77
Delicious Pot Roast, 69
Fajitas with Grilled Vegetables, 63
▶ Famous Corn Chip Pie, 64
Hallie's Skillet Dried Beef & Corn, 42
Inside-Out Stuffed Pepper, 24
Mom's Spaghetti & Meatballs, 81
One-Pot Beef Ravioli, 53
Ramen Skillet Supper, 35
Saucy Beef Skillet, 25
Skillet Bowtie Lasagna, 61
Skillet Goulash, 52
Sloppy Cowboys, 16
Southwestern Corn Skillet, 99
Stovetop Beef & Shells, 37
Stroganoff-Style Steak, 39
Super-Simple Swiss Steak, 74
▶ Taco in a Pan, 85

Fish & Seafood

BBQ Shrimp & Pineapple Kabobs, 22
Coconut Mahi-Mahi, 95
Grilled Tilapia with Pineapple Salsa, 98
Kickin' Cajun Tilapia, 19
Low-Country Shrimp Boil, 55
Maryland Crab Cakes, 87

Picture-Perfect Paella, 71
Seafood Linguine with a Kick, 105
Shrimp & Orzo Salad, 20
Sole in Dill Butter, 34

Pork

Bowties, Sausage & Beans, 97
Creole Pork Chops & Rice, 40
Family-Favorite Pork Tacos, 13
Farmhouse Pork & Cabbage Sauté, 48
Grilled Sausage & Veggie Packs, 88
Ham & Potato Skillet Supper, 96
Hearty Red Beans & Rice, 28
Pepperoni Tortellini, 45
Pork Chops Olé, 75
Sausage Patties & Marinara Sauce, 92
Savory Beans & Tomatoes over Rice, 101
So-Easy Pork Fritters, 11
Southwest Smoked Sausage Skillet, 33
Spicy Sausage & Rice, 15
Sweet Skillet Ham Steak & Apples, 29
Too-Much-Zucchini Stovetop Dinner, 26
Ziti with Sausage & Zucchini, 41

Poultry

Amanda's Chicken & Orzo, 31
Aunt Annie's Chicken Paprika, 62
Barbecue Chicken Kabobs, 7
Buttermilk Fried Chicken, 54
Chicken & Snow Pea Stir-Fry, 21
Chicken Cranberry Ruby, 79

INDEX

Chicken Romano, 9
Chicken-Rice Skillet, 56
Creamed Chicken on Biscuits, 104
Curried Chicken with Mango, 100
Easy One-Pot Chicken & Rice, 12
Fluffy Chicken & Dumplings, 70
Garden Skillet Dinner with Chicken, 18
Honey Chicken & Carrots, 44
Mom's Chicken Riggies, 102
Mom's Cola Chicken, 72
One-Dish Speedy Couscous, 8
Pasta a la Drini, 49
Pulled Chicken & Slaw Sandwiches, 50
Quick Coq au Vin, 66
Rosemary Chicken & Tomatoes, 73
Skillet Chicken-Fried Rice, 14
Speedy Chicken Gumbo, 84
Spinach & Provolone-Stuffed Chicken, 68
Tempting Teriyaki Chicken, 78
Tomato & Chicken Penne, 91

Soups

Basil & Tomato Soup, 10
Chicken & Apple Wild Rice Soup, 60
Creamy Pumpkin Soup, 65
Creamy White Chili, 86
Dijon Beef Stew, 57
Hearty Sausage Soup, 51
Hunting Cabin Chili, 89
Meatball Soup, 17

New England Fish Chowder, 90
One-Pot Spicy Black Bean Chili, 43
Sunday Meeting Tomato Soup, 93
Tortilla Stew, 80
Zucchini & Seashells Soup, 32

Sweet Treats

Chocolate Oatmeal Cookies, 46
Chocolate-Hazelnut Skillet Bars, 82
Coconutty Nanaimo Bars, 83
Pineapple Pudding, 107
Simple Skillet Peaches, 106
Skillet Strawberry Jam, 47

Veggie

Basil-Broccoli Pasta, 30
Black-Eyed Peas & Potato Skillet, 58
Lucky-7 Mac & Cheese, 94
Pasta Puttanesca, 38
Pasta Trapanese, 76
Rosemary Peppers & Fusilli, 23
Vegetable Quesadillas, 27

So-Easy Pork Fritters, *page 11*

One-Dish Speedy Couscous, *page 8*

Bowties, Sausage & Beans, *page 97*

Picture-Perfect Paella, *page 71*

Our Story

Back in 1984, we were next-door neighbors raising our families in the little town of Delaware, Ohio. Two moms with small children, we were looking for a way to do what we loved and stay home with the kids too. We had always shared a love of home cooking and making memories with family & friends and so, after many a conversation over the backyard fence, **Gooseberry Patch** was born.

We put together our first catalog at our kitchen tables, enlisting the help of our loved ones wherever we could. From that very first mailing, we found an immediate connection with many of our customers and it wasn't long before we began receiving letters, photos and recipes from these new friends. In 1992, we put together our very first cookbook, compiled from hundreds of these recipes and, the rest, as they say, is history.

Hard to believe it's been over 25 years since those kitchen-table days! From that original little **Gooseberry Patch** family, we've grown to include an amazing group of creative folks who love cooking, decorating and creating as much as we do. Today, we're best known for our homestyle, family-friendly cookbooks, now recognized as national bestsellers.

JoAnn & Vickie

One thing's for sure, we couldn't have done it without our friends all across the country. Each year, we're honored to turn thousands of your recipes into our collectible cookbooks. Our hope is that each book captures the stories and heart of all of you who have shared with us. Whether you've been with us since the beginning or are just discovering us, welcome to the **Gooseberry Patch** family!

Visit us online:
www.gooseberrypatch.com
1·800·854·6673

U.S. to Metric Recipe Equivalents

Volume Measurements

1/4 teaspoon	1 mL
1/2 teaspoon	2 mL
1 teaspoon	5 mL
1 tablespoon = 3 teaspoons	15 mL
2 tablespoons = 1 fluid ounce	30 mL
1/4 cup	60 mL
1/3 cup	75 mL
1/2 cup = 4 fluid ounces	125 mL
1 cup = 8 fluid ounces	250 mL
2 cups = 1 pint =16 fluid ounces	500 mL
4 cups = 1 quart	1 L

Weights

1 ounce	30 g
4 ounces	120 g
8 ounces	225 g
16 ounces = 1 pound	450 g

Oven Temperatures

300° F	150° C
325° F	160° C
350° F	180° C
375° F	190° C
400° F	200° C
450° F	230° C

Baking Pan Sizes

Square

8x8x2 inches	2 L = 20x20x5 cm
9x9x2 inches	2.5 L = 23x23x5 cm

Rectangular

13x9x2 inches	3.5 L = 33x23x5 cm

Loaf

9x5x3 inches	2 L = 23x13x7 cm

Round

8x1-1/2 inches	1.2 L = 20x4 cm
9x1-1/2 inches	1.5 L = 23x4 cm

Recipe Abbreviations

t. = teaspoon	ltr. = liter
T. = tablespoon	oz. = ounce
c. = cup	lb. = pound
pt. = pint	doz. = dozen
qt. = quart	pkg. = package
gal. = gallon	env. = envelope

Kitchen Measurements

A pinch = 1/8 tablespoon	1 fluid ounce = 2 tablespoons
3 teaspoons = 1 tablespoon	4 fluid ounces = 1/2 cup
2 tablespoons = 1/8 cup	8 fluid ounces = 1 cup
4 tablespoons = 1/4 cup	16 fluid ounces = 1 pint
8 tablespoons = 1/2 cup	32 fluid ounces = 1 quart
16 tablespoons = 1 cup	16 ounces net weight = 1 pound
2 cups = 1 pint	
4 cups = 1 quart	
4 quarts = 1 gallon	